Christianity and Progress

By

Harry Emerson Fosdick

Christianity and Progress

LECTURE I

THE IDEA OF PROGRESS

I

The supposition that fish do not recognize the existence of water nor birds the existence of air often has been used to illustrate the insensitive unawareness of which we all are capable in the presence of some encompassing medium of our lives. The illustration aptly fits the minds of multitudes in this generation, who live, as we all do, in the atmosphere of progressive hopes and yet are not intelligently aware of it nor conscious of its newness, its strangeness and its penetrating influence. We read as a matter of course such characteristic lines as these from Tennyson:

"Yet I doubt not thro' the ages one increasing purpose runs,

And the thoughts of men are widen'd with the process of the suns."

Such lines, however, are not to be taken as a matter of course; until comparatively recent generations such an idea as that never had dawned on anybody's mind, and the story of the achievement of that progressive interpretation of history is one of the most fascinating narratives in the long record of man's mental Odyssey. In particular, the Christian who desires to understand the influences, both intellectual and practical, which are playing with transforming power upon Christianity today, upon its doctrines, its purposes, its institutions, and its social applications, must first of all understand the idea of progress. For like a changed climate, which in time alters the fauna and flora of a continent beyond the power of human conservatism to resist, this progressive conception of life is affecting every thought and purpose of man, and no attempted segregation of religion from its influence is likely to succeed.

The significance of this judgment becomes the more clear when we note the fact that the idea of progress in our modern sense is not to be found before the sixteenth century. Men before that time had lived without progressive hopes just as before Copernicus they had lived upon a stationary earth.

Man's life was not thought of as a growth; gradual change for the better was not supposed to be God's method with mankind; the future was not conceived in terms of possible progress; and man's estate on earth was not looked upon as capable of indefinite perfectibility. All these ideas, so familiar to us, were undreamed of in the ancient and medieval world. The new astronomy is not a more complete break from the old geocentric system with its stationary earth than is our modern progressive way of thinking from our fathers' static conception of human life and history.

II

It will be worth our while at the beginning of our study to review in outline this development of the idea of progress, that we may better understand the reasons for its emergence and may more truly estimate its revolutionary effects. In the ancient world the Greeks, with all their far-flung speculations, never hit upon the idea of progress. To be sure, clear intimations, scattered here and there in Greek literature, indicate faith that man in the past had improved his lot. Aeschylus saw men lifted from their hazardous lives in sunless caves by the intervention of Prometheus and his sacrificial teaching of the arts of peace; Euripides contrasted the primitive barbarism in which man began with the civilized estate which in Greece he had achieved—but this perceived advance never was erected into a progressive idea of human life as a whole. Rather, the original barbarism, from which the arts of civilization had for a little lifted men, was itself a degeneration from a previous ideal estate, and human history as a whole was a cyclic and repetitious story of never-ending rise and fall. Plato's philosophy of history was typical: the course of cosmic life is divided into cycles, each seventy-two thousand solar years in length; during the first half of each cycle, when creation newly comes from the hands of Deity, mankind's estate is happily ideal, but then decay begins and each cycle's latter half sinks from bad to worse until Deity once more must take a hand and make all things new again. Indeed, so far from reaching the idea of progress, the ancient Greeks at the very center of their thinking were incapacitated for such an achievement by their suspiciousness of change. They were artists and to them the perfect was finished, like the Parthenon, and therefore was incapable of being improved by change. Change, so far from meaning, as it does with us, the possibility of betterment, meant with them the certainty of decay; no changes upon earth in the long run were good; all change was the sure sign that the period of degeneration had set in from which only divine intervention could redeem mankind. Paul on Mars Hill quoted the Greek poet Aratus concerning the sonship of all mankind to God, but Aratus's philosophy of history is not so pleasantly quotable:

"How base a progeny sprang from golden sires!

And viler shall they be whom ye beget."

Such, in general, was the non-progressive outlook of the ancient Greeks.

Nor did the Romans hit upon the idea of progress in any form remotely approaching our modern meaning. The casual reader, to be sure, will find occasional flares of expectancy about the future or of pride in the advance of the past which at first suggest progressive interpretations of history. So Seneca, rejoicing because he thought he knew the explanation of the moon's eclipses, wrote: "The days will come when those things which now lie hidden time and human diligence will bring to light. . . . The days will come when our posterity will marvel that we were ignorant of truths so obvious." So, too, the Epicureans, like the Greek tragedians before them, believed that human knowledge and effort had lifted mankind out of primitive barbarism and Lucretius described how man by the development of agriculture and navigation, the building of cities and the establishment of laws, the manufacture of physical conveniences and the creation of artistic beauty, had risen, "gradually progressing," to his present height. Such hopeful changes in the past, however, were not the prophecies of continuous advance; they were but incidental fluctuations in a historic process which knew no progress as a whole. Even the Stoics saw in history only a recurrent rise and fall in endless repetition so that all apparent change for good or evil was but the influx or the ebbing of the tide in an essentially unchanging sea. The words of Marcus Aurelius are typical: "The periodic movements of the universe are the same, up and down from age to age"; "He who has seen present things has seen all, both everything which has taken place from all eternity and everything which will be for time without end; for all are of one kin and of one form"; "He who is forty years old, if he has any understanding at all, has, by virtue of the uniformity that prevails, seen all things which have been and all that will be."

When with these Greek and Roman ideas the Hebrew-Christian influences blended, no conception of progress in the modern sense was added by the Church's contribution. To be sure, the Christians' uncompromising faith in personality as the object of divine redemption and their vigorous hope about the future of God's people in the next world, if not in this, calcined some elements in the classical tradition. Belief in cycles, endlessly repeating themselves through cosmic ages, went by the board. This earth became the theatre of a unique experiment made once for all; in place of the ebb and flow of tides in a changeless sea, mankind's story became a drama moving toward a climactic denouement that would shake heaven and earth together in a divine cataclysm. But this consummation of all history was not a goal progressively to be achieved; it was a divine invasion of the world expectantly to be awaited, when the victorious Christ would return and the Day of Judgment dawn.

The development of this apocalyptic phrasing of hope has been traced too often to require long rehearsal here. If the Greeks were essentially philosophers and welcomed congenially ideas like endless cosmic cycles, the Hebrews were essentially practical and dramatic in their thinking and they welcomed a picture of God's victory capable of being visualized by the imagination. At first their national hopes had been set on the restoration of the Davidic kingdom; then the Davidic king himself had grown in their imagination until, as Messiah in a proper sense, he gathered to himself supernal attributes; then, as a child of their desperate national circumstances, the hope was born of their Messiah's sudden coming on the clouds of heaven for their help. Between the Testaments this expectation expanded and robed itself with pomp and glory, so that when the Christians came they found awaiting them a phrasing of hope which they accepted to body forth their certainty of God's coming sovereignty over all the earth. This expectation of coming triumph was not progressive; it was cataclysmic. It did not offer the prospect of great gains to be worked for over long periods of time; it offered a divine invasion of history immediately at hand. It was pictured, not in terms of human betterment to be achieved, but of divine action to be awaited. The victory would suddenly come like the flood in Noah's day, like the lightning flashing from one end of the heaven to the other, like a thief in the night.

To be sure, this eager expectation of a heavenly kingdom immediately to arrive on earth soon grew dim among the Christians, and the reasons are obvious. For one thing, the Church herself, moving out from days of hardship to days of preferment and prosperity, began to allure with her inviting prospects of growing power the enthusiasms and hopes of the people, until not the suddenly appearing kingdom from the heavens, but the expanding Church on earth became the center of Christian interest. For another thing, Christ meant more to Christians than the inaugurator of a postponed kingdom which, long awaited with ardent expectation, still did not arrive; Christ was the giver of eternal life now. More and more the emphasis shifted from what Christ would do for his people when he came upon the clouds of heaven to what he was doing for them through his spiritual presence with them. Even in the Fourth Gospel one finds this good news that Christ had already come again in the hearts of his people insisted on in evident contrast with the apocalyptic hope literally conceived. For another thing, dramatic hopes of a sudden invasion of the world are always the offspring of desperate conditions. Only when people are hard put to it do they want history catastrophically stopped in the midst of its course. The Book of Daniel must be explained by the tyrannies of Antiochus Epiphanes, the Book of Revelation by the persecutions of Domitian, the present recrudescence of pre-millennialism by the tragedy of the Great War. But when the persecution of the Church by the State gave way to the running of the State by the Church; when to be a Christian was no longer a road to the lions but the sine qua non of preferment and power; when the souls under the altar ceased crying, "How long, O Master, the holy and true, dost thou not judge and avenge our blood on them that dwell on the earth?" then the apocalyptic hopes grew dim and the old desire for a kingdom immediately to come was subdued to an expectation, no longer imperative and urgent, that sometime the course of history would stop on Judgment Day.

In all these Greek and Roman, Hebrew and Christian contributions, which flowed together and then flowed out into the medieval age, there was no suggestion of a modern idea of progress, and in the medieval age itself there was nothing to create a fresh phrasing of expectancy. Men were aware of the darkness of the days that had fallen on the earth; even when they began to rouse themselves from their lethargy, their thoughts of greatness did not reach forward toward a golden age ahead but harked back

"To the glory that was Greece

And the grandeur that was Rome,"

and their intellectual life, instead of being an adventurous search for new truth, was a laborious endeavour to stabilize the truth already formulated in the great days of the early Church. Indeed, the Church's specific contribution of a vividly imagined faith in a future world, as the goal of the most absorbing hopes and fears of men, tended rather to confirm than to dissipate the static conception of earthly life and history. With an urgency that the ancient world had never known the Christian world believed in immortality and visualized the circumstances of the life to come so concretely that in a medieval catechism the lurid colour of the setting sun was ascribed to the supposition that "he looketh down upon hell." Nothing in this life had any importance save as it prepared the souls of men for life to come. Even Roger Bacon, his mind flashing like a beacon from below the sky-line of the modern world, was sure that all man's knowledge of nature was useful only in preparing his soul to await the coming of Antichrist and the Day of Judgment. There was no idea of progress, then, in the medieval age. Human life and history were static and the only change to be anticipated was the climactic event

"When earth breaks up and heaven expands."

III

The emergence of modern progressive hopes out of this static medievalism is one of the epic occurrences of history. The causes which furthered the movement seem now in retrospect to be woven into a fabric so tightly meshed as to resist unraveling. Nevertheless, it is not difficult to see at least some of the major factors which furthered this revolutionary change from a static to a progressive world.

Among the first, scientific invention is surely to be noted. Even Roger Bacon, prophecying with clairvoyant insight far in advance of the event, foresaw one of the determining factors of the modern age: "Machines for navigating can be made so that without rowers great ships can be guided by one pilot on river or sea more swiftly than if they were full of oarsmen. Likewise vehicles are possible which without draught-animals can be propelled with incredible speed, like the scythed chariots, as we picture them, in which antiquity fought. Likewise a flying machine is possible in the middle of which a man may sit, using some ingenious device by which artificial wings will beat the air like those of a flying bird. Also machines, small in size, can be constructed to lift and move unlimited weights, than which in an emergency nothing is more useful." So dreamed the great friar in the thirteenth century. When, then, we find the minds of men first throwing off their intellectual vassalage to antiquity and beginning to believe in themselves, their present powers and their future prospects, it is this new-found mastery over nature's latent resources which is the spring and fountain of their confidence. Cardan, in the sixteenth century, marveling at the then modern inventions of the compass, the printing press, and gunpowder, cried, "All antiquity has nothing comparable to these three things." Every year from that day to this has deepened the impression made upon the minds of men by the marvelous prospect of harnessing the resources of the universe. The last one hundred and twenty-five years have seen the invention of the locomotive, the steamship, the telegraph, the sewing machine, the camera, the telephone, the gasoline engine, wireless telegraphy and telephony, and the many other applications of electricity. As one by one new areas of power have thus come under the control of man, with every conquest suggesting many more not yet achieved but brought within range of possibility, old theories of cosmic degeneration and circular futility have gone to pieces, the glamour of antiquity has lost its allurement, the great days of humanity upon the earth have been projected into the future, and the gradual achievement of human progress has become the hope of man.

Another element in the emergence of the modern progressive outlook upon life is immediately consequent upon the first: world-wide discovery, exploration and intercommunication. Great as the practical results have been which trace their source to the adventurers who, from Columbus down, pioneered unknown seas to unknown lands, the psychological effects have been greater still. Who could longer live cooped up in a static world, when the old barriers were so being overpassed and new continents were inviting adventure, settlement, and social experiment hitherto untried? The theological progressiveness of the Pilgrim Fathers, starting out from Leyden for a new world, was not primarily a matter of speculation; it was even more a matter of an adventurous spirit, which, once admitted into life, could not be kept out of religious thought as well. In Edward Winslow's account of Pastor Robinson's last sermon before the little company of pioneers left Leyden, we read that Robinson "took occasion also miserably to bewaile the state and condition of the Reformed Churches, who were come to a period in Religion, and would goe no further than the instruments of their Reformation: As for example, the Lutherans they could not be drawne to goe beyond what Luther saw, for whatever part of God's will he had further imparted and revealed to Calvin, they will die rather than embrace it. And so also, saith he, you see the Calvinists, they stick where he left them: a misery much to bee lamented; For though they were precious shining lights in their times, yet God hath not revealed his whole will to them: And were they now living, saith hee, they would bee as ready and willing to embrace further light, as that they had received." Static methods of thinking are here evidently going to pieces before the impact of a distinctly unstatic world. They were looking for "more truth and light yet to breake forth out of his holy Word" because they lived in a time when new things had been happening at an exhilarating rate and when pioneering adventure and general travel in a world of open avenues were already beginning to have that liberating effect which has increased with every passing century.

Closely allied with the two elements already noted is a third: the increase of knowledge, which, as in the case of astronomy, threw discredit upon the superior claims of antiquity and made modern men seem wiser than their sires. For ages the conviction had held the ground that the ancients were the wisest men who ever lived and that we, their children, were but infants in comparison. When, therefore, the Copernican astronomy proved true, when the first terrific shock of it had passed through resultant anger into wonder and from wonder into stupefied acceptance, and from that at last into amazed exultation at the vast, new universe unveiled, the credit of antiquity received a stunning blow. So far was Aristotle from being "the master of those who know" whom the medievalists had revered, that he had not even known the shape and motion of the earth or its relation with the sun. For the first time in history the idea emerged that humanity accumulates knowledge, that the ancients were the infants, that the moderns represent the age and wisdom of the race. Consider the significance of those words of Pascal in the seventeenth century: "Those whom we call ancient were really new in all things, and properly constituted the infancy of mankind; and as we have joined to their knowledge the experience of the centuries which have followed them, it is in ourselves that we should find this antiquity that we revere in others." For the first time in history men turned their faces, in their search for knowledge, not backward but forward, and began to experience that attitude which with us is habitual—standing on tip-toe in eager expectancy, sure that tomorrow some new and unheard of truth will be revealed.

New inventions, new discoveries, new knowledge—even before the eighteenth century all these factors were under way. Then a new factor entered which has played a powerful part in substituting a progressive for a static world: new social hopes. The medieval age had no expectation of a better social life on earth. Charity was common but it was purely individual and remedial; it did not seek to understand or to cure the causes of social maladjustment; it was sustained by no expectation of better conditions among men; it was valued because of the giver's unselfishness rather than because of the recipient's gain, and in consequence it was for the most part unregulated alms-giving, piously motivated but inefficiently managed. In the eighteenth century a new outlook and hope emerged. If man could pioneer new lands, learn new truth and make new inventions, why could he not devise new social systems where human life would be freed from the miseries of misgovernment and oppression? With that question at last definitely rising, the long line of social reformers began which stretched from Abbé de Saint-Pierre to the latest believer in the possibility of a more decent and salutary social life for human-kind. The coming of democracy in government incalculably stimulated the influence of this social hope, for with the old static forms of absolute autocracy now broken up, with power in the hands of the people to seek as they would "life, liberty and the pursuit of happiness," who could put limits to the possibilities? The medieval age was gone; the modern age had come, and its distinctive note was progress, with new inventions, new discoveries, new knowledge and new social hope.

It would be a fascinating task to watch these interweaving factors at their work and to trace their commingled influence as slowly their involved significance became clear, now to this man and now to that. The best narrative that has been written yet of this epochal movement is contained in Professor Bury's volume on "The Idea of Progress." There one sees the stream of this progressive conception of life pushing its way out as through a delta by way of many minds, often far separated yet flowing with the same water. Some men attacked the ancients and by comparison praised the modern time as Perrault did with "The Age of Louis the Great"; some men foresaw so clearly the possibility of man's control over nature that they dreamed of terrestrial Utopias as Francis Bacon did in "New Atlantis"; some men, like Descartes, sought to grasp the intellectual conditions of human improvement; and others, like Condorcet, became the fervid prophets of human perfectibility; some, like Turgot, re-examined history in terms of the new ideas; and some, like Saint Simon and Comte, sought to discover the law by which all progress moves. This new idea of life and history came "by divers portions and in divers manners," but no one can doubt its arrival. The life of man upon this earth was no longer conceived as static; it was progressive and the possibilities that lay ahead made all the achievements of the past seem like the play of childhood.

At last, in the nineteenth century, the climactic factor was added which gathered up all the rest and embraced them in a comprehensive philosophy of life. Evolution became a credible truth. No longer a dim conjecture, it was established in biology, and then it spread its influence out into every area of human thought until all history was conceived in genetic terms and all the sciences were founded upon the evolutionary idea. Growth became recognized as the fundamental law of life. Nothing in the universe without, or in man's life within, could longer be conceived as having sprung full-statured, like Minerva from the head of Jove. All things achieved maturity by gradual processes. The world itself had thus come into being, not artificially nailed together like a box, but growing like a tree, putting forth ever new branches and new leaves. When this idea had firmly grasped the human mind, the modern age had come indeed, and progress was its distinctive category of understanding and its exhilarating phrasing of human hope. Then came the days of mid-Victorian optimism with songs like this upon men's lips:

"Every tiger madness muzzled, every serpent passion kill'd,

Every grim ravine a garden, every blazing desert till'd,

"Robed in universal harvest up to either pole she smiles,

Universal ocean softly washing all her warless isles."

IV

Any one, however, who has lived with discerning thought through the opening years of the twentieth century, must be aware that something has happened to chasten and subdue these wildly enthusiastic hopes of the mid-Victorian age. Others beside the "gloomy dean" of St. Paul's, whether through well-considered thought or through the psychological shock of the Great War, have come to look upon this rash, unmitigated enthusiasm about the earth's future as a fool's paradise. At any rate, no treatment of the idea of progress would be complete which did not dwell upon the limitations to that idea, now definitely obvious to thoughtful men.

As early as 1879, in Saporta's "Le Monde des Plantes," we run upon one serious setback to unqualified expectations of progress. Men began to take into account the fact that this earth is not a permanent affair. "We recognize from this point of view as from others," wrote Saporta, "that the world was once young; then adolescent; that it has even passed the age of maturity; man has come late, when a beginning of physical decadence had struck the globe, his domain." Here is a fact to give enthusiasm over earthly progress serious pause. This earth, once uninhabitable, will be uninhabitable again. If not by wholesale catastrophe, then by the slow wearing down of the sun's heat, already passed its climacteric, this planet, the transient theatre of the human drama, will be no longer the scene of man's activity, but as cold as the moon, or as hot as colliding stars in heaven, will be able to sustain human life no more. "The grandest material works of the human race," wrote Faye in 1884, "will have to be effaced by degrees under the action of a few physical forces which will survive man for a time. Nothing will remain, not even the ruins."

Every suggested clew to a possible escape from the grimness of the planet's dissolution has been followed up with careful search. The discovery of radioactivity seemed to promise endlessly extended life to our sun, but Sir E. Rutherford, before the Royal Astronomical Society, has roundly denied that the discovery materially lengthens our estimate of the sun's tenure of life and has said that if the sun were made of uranium it would not because of that last five years the longer as a giver of heat. Whether we will or not, we have no choice except to face the tremendous fact, calmly set down by von Hartmann in 1904: "The only question is whether . . . the world-process will work itself out slowly in prodigious lapse of time, according to purely physical laws; or whether it will find its end by means of some metaphysical resource when it has reached its culminating point. Only in the last case would its end coincide with the fulfilment of a purpose or object; in the first case, a long period of purposeless existence would follow after the culmination of life."

In a word, men delighted at the prospect of human progress on this planet have made an idol of it, only to discover that on a transient earth it leads nowhere without God and immortality. One disciple of naturalism recently denied his desire to believe in God because he wanted a risky universe. But the universe without God is not risky; it is a foregone conclusion; the dice are all loaded. After the lapse of millions of years which, however long they be stretched out, will ultimately end, our solar system will be gone, without even a memory left of anything that ever was dreamed or done within it. That is the inevitable issue of such a "risky" universe. When scientifically-minded men, therefore, now take a long look ahead, the Utopian visions of the mid-Victorian age are not foremost in their thought. Rather, as one of them recently wrote:

"One is tempted to imagine this race of supermen, of some millions of years hence, grimly confronting the issue of extinction. Probably long before that time science will have perfectly mastered the problem of the sun's heat, and will be able to state precisely at what period the radiation will sink to a level which would normally be fatal to the living inhabitants of the planets. Then will begin the greatest of cosmic events: a drama that has doubtless been played numbers of times already on the stage of the universe: the last stand of the wonderful microcosm against the brute force of the macrocosm. . . . .

"One conceives that our supermen will face the end philosophically. Death is losing its terrors. The race will genially say, as we individuals do to-day, that it has had a long run. But it will none-the-less make a grim fight. Life will be worth living, for everybody, long before that consummation is in sight. The hovering demon of cold and darkness will be combatted by scientific means of which we have not the germ of a conception."

If ever a river ran out into a desert, the river of progressive hopes, fed only from springs of materialistic philosophy, has done so here. At least the Greeks had their immortality and the Hebrews their coming Kingdom of God, but a modern materialist, with all his talk of progress, has neither the one nor the other, nor anything to take their place as an ultimate for hope. Whatever else may be true, progress on a transient planet has not done away with the need of God and life eternal.

Moreover, not only have our twentieth century thought and experience seriously qualified the meaning of progress on this earth by the limiting of the earth's duration; men have come also to distrust, as a quite unjustified flourish of sentimentality, the mid-Victorian confidence in an automatic evolution which willy-nilly lifts humanity to higher levels. Said Herbert Spencer, "Progress is not an accident, not a thing within human control, but a beneficent necessity." "This advancement is due to the working of a universal law; . . . in virtue of that law it must continue until the state we call perfection is reached. . . . Thus the ultimate development of the ideal man is logically certain — as certain as any conclusion in which we place the most implicit faith; . . . so surely must the things we call evil and immorality disappear; so surely must man become perfect." There is no scientific basis whatever for such a judgment. Evolution is not an escalator which, whether or not man run in addition to its lift, will inevitably raise humanity to a heaven on earth. Potatoes in the cellar shooting out long white eyes in search of light are evolving, but they are evolving worse. Upon the basis of a scientific doctrine of evolution, no idolatrous superstition could be much more lacking in intellectual support than Spencer's confidence in a universal, mechanical, irresistible movement toward perfection. The plain fact is that human history is a strange blend of progress and regress; it is the story of the rhythmic rise and fall of civilizations and empires, of gains made only to be lost and lost only to be fought for once again. Even when advance has come, it has come by mingled progress and cataclysm as water passes, through gradual increase of warmth, from ice suddenly to liquid and from liquid suddenly to vapour. Our nineteenth century ideas of evolution tended to create in us the impression that humanity had made a smooth and even ascent. We artificially graded the ascending track of human history, leveled and macadamized it, and talked of inevitable progress. Such sentimental optimism has ceased even to be comforting, so utterly untenable has it become to every well-instructed mind.

To such unfounded faith in automatic progress a valuable counterweight is acquaintance with the life of a man like St. Augustine. As one reads Augustine's sermons one can hear in the background the collapse of a great civilization. One can tell from his discourses when the barbarians began to move on Rome. One can hear the crash when Alaric and his hordes sacked the Eternal City. One can catch the accent of horror at the tidal waves of anarchy that everywhere swept in to engulf the falling empire. "Horrible things," said Augustine, "have been told us. There have been ruins, and fires, and rapine, and murder, and torture. That is true; we have heard it many times; we have shuddered at all this disaster; we have often wept, and we have hardly been able to console ourselves." At last, the empire in ruins, the old civilization tottering to its collapse, Augustine died in his episcopal city of Hippo, while the barbarians were hammering at the city gates. Through such scenes this generation too has lived and has had to learn again, what we never should have forgotten, that human history is not a smooth and well-rolled lawn of soft ascents; that it is mountainous, precipitous, terrific—a country where all progress must be won by dint of intelligence and toil, and where it is as easy to lose the gains of civilization as it is to fall over a cliff or to surrender a wheat field to the weeds. An archeologist in Mesopotamia talked with an Arab lad who neither read, himself, nor knew any one who did; yet the lad, when he acknowledged this, stood within a stone's throw of the site where milleniums ago was one of the greatest universities of the ancient world and where still, amid the desolation, one could dig and find the old clay tablets on which the children of that ancient time had learned to write. Progress? Regress! While history as a whole, from the Cro-Magnon man to the twentieth century, does certainly suggest a great ascent, it has not been an automatic levitation. It has been a fight, tragic and ceaseless, against destructive forces. This world needs something more than a soft gospel of inevitable progress. It needs salvation from its ignorance, its sin, its inefficiency, its apathy, its silly optimisms and its appalling carelessness.

V

Nevertheless, though it is true that our modern ideas of progress on this earth never in themselves can supply an adequate philosophy of life, and though it is true that they do not dispense with, but rather emphasize, our need of God and immortality and the saving powers which Christians find in Christ, yet those ideas have in them a permanent contribution to the life of man from whose influence the race cannot escape. When we have granted the limitations which disillusioned thoughtfulness suggests concerning progress upon this earth, it still remains true that, in our new scientific control over the latent resources of the earth without and over our own mental and moral processes within, we have a machinery for producing change that opens up exciting prospects before humanity. Never in our outlook upon man's earthly future can we go back to the endless cosmic cycles of the Greeks or the apocalyptic expectations of the Hebrews. We are committed to the hope of making progress, and the central problem which Christianity faces in adjusting her thought and practice to the modern age is the problem of coming to intelligent terms with this dominant idea.

These lectures are an excursion to spy out this land and to see, if we may, what the idea of progress through the scientific control of life is likely to mean and ought to mean to Christianity. If this modern idea is not intelligently guided in its effect upon our faith and practice, it will none the less have its effect in haphazard, accidental, unguided, and probably ruinous ways. If one listens, for example, to the preaching of liberal ministers, one sees that every accent of their teaching has been affected by this prevalent and permeating thought. The God they preach no longer sits afar like Dante's deity in the stationary empyrean beyond all reach of change; their God is here in the midst of the human struggle, "their Captain in the well-fought fight." H. G. Wells may be a poor theologian but he is one of our best interpreters of popular thought and his idea of God, marching through the world "like fifes and drums," calling the people to a progressive crusade for righteousness, is one which modern folk find it most easy to accept. He is a God of progress who undergirds our endeavours for justice in the earth with his power; who fights in and for and with us against the hosts of evil; whose presence is a guarantee of ultimate victory; and whose effect upon us is to send us out to war against ancient human curses, assured that what ought to be done can be done.

As men's thought of God has thus been molded by the idea of progress on the earth, so, too, the Christ they preach is not primarily, as of old, the victim by whose substitutionary sacrifice the race of men has found an open door from the bottomless pit of endless woe to a blessed immortality in Paradise. The modern emphasis is all another way. Christ is the divine revealer whose spirit alone can transform individuals and save society. The sort of character he was, the life he lived, the ideas he promulgated, are the salt that can preserve human life, the light that can illumine the way to a kingdom of righteousness on earth. He himself is the leader in the fight for that kingdom, his sacrifice part of the price it costs, his spirit the quality of life that is indispensable to its coming, and when we think of him we sing,

"The Son of God goes forth to war. . . .

Who follows in his train?"

So, too, the Church, as presented by typical modern preachers, is no longer an ark to which, from the flood of wrath divine, the few may flee for safety. If men tried to preach in that way, the message would stick in their throats. The Church is primarily an instrument in God's hands to bring personal and social righteousness upon the earth. When her massed influence overcomes a public evil or establishes a public good, men find the justification of her existence and a first-rate weapon of apologetic argument in her behalf. When wars come, the Church is blamed because she did not prevent them; when wars are over, she takes counsel how she may prove the validity of her message by making their recurrence impossible; and the pitiful dismemberment of the Church by sects and schisms is hated and deplored, not so much because of economic waste or theological folly, as because these insane divisions prevent social effectiveness in bringing the message of Christ to bear influentially on modern life.

Likewise, hope, deeply affected by modern ideas of earthly progress, is not primarily post-mortem, as it used to be. Men believe in immortality, but it seems so naturally the continuance of this present life that their responsible concern is chiefly centered here. The hopes which waken immediate enthusiasm and stir spontaneous response are hopes of righteousness victorious upon the earth. Because men believe in God, they believe that he has great purposes for humankind. The course of human history is like a river: sometimes it flows so slowly that one would hardly know it moved at all; sometimes bends come in its channel so that one can hardly see in what direction it intends to go; sometimes there are back-eddies so that it seems to be retreating on itself. If a man has no spiritual interpretation of life, if he does not believe in God, he may well give up hope and conclude that the human river is flowing all awry or has altogether ceased to move. A Christian, however, has a spiritual interpretation of life. He knows that human history is a river—not a whirlpool, nor a pond, but a river flowing to its end. Just as, far inland, we can tell that the Hudson is flowing to the sea, because the waters, when the tide comes in, are tinctured with the ocean's quality, so now, we believe that we can tell that the river of human history is flowing out toward the kingdom of our God. Already the setback of the divine ocean is felt among us in ideals of better life, personal, social, economic, national. That it is Christianity's function to believe in these ideals, to have faith in the possibility of their realization, to supply motives for their achievement, and to work for them with courage and sacrifice, is the familiar note of modern Christian hope.

The modern apologetic also is tinctured with this same quality. Not as of old is it a laboured working out of metaphysical propositions. Rather, a modern Christian preacher's defense of the Gospel may be paraphrased in some such strain as this: You never can achieve a decent human life upon this planet apart from the Christian Gospel. Neither outward economic comfort nor international treaties of peace can save the day for humanity. Not even when our present situation is described as "a race between education and catastrophe" has the case been adequately stated. What kind of education is meant? If every man and woman on earth were a Ph. D., would that solve the human problem? Aaron Burr had a far keener intellect than George Washington. So far as swiftness and agility of intelligence were concerned, Burr far out-distanced the slow-pacing mind of

Washington. But, for all that, as you watch Burr's life, and many another's like him, you understand what Macaulay meant when he exclaimed: "as if history were not made up of the bad actions of extraordinary men, as if all the most noted destroyers and deceivers of our species, all the founders of arbitrary governments and false religions, had not been extraordinary men, as if nine tenths of the calamities which have befallen the human race had any other origin than the union of high intelligence with low desires." Was Nebuchadnezzar of Babylon unintelligent? Caesar and Napoleon—were they unintelligent? Has the most monumental and destructive selfishness in human history been associated with poor minds? No, with great minds, which, if the world was to be saved their devastation, needed to be reborn into a new spirit. The transforming gospel which religion brings is indispensable to a building of the kingdom of righteousness upon the earth.

Wherever one listens, then, to the typical teaching of modern Christians, he finds himself in the atmosphere of the idea of progress. Men's thoughts of God, of Christ, of the Church, of hope, their methods of apologetic, are shaped to that mold—are often thinned out and flattened down and made cheap and unconvincing by being shaped to that mold—so that an endeavour to achieve an intelligent understanding of Christianity's relationship with the idea of progress is in part a defensive measure to save the Gospel from being unintelligently mauled and mishandled by it. Marcus Dods, when he was an old man, said: "I do not envy those who have to fight the battle of Christianity in the twentieth century." Then, after a moment, he added, "Yes, perhaps I do, but it will be a stiff fight." It is a stiff fight, and for this reason if for no other, that before we can get on much further in a progressive world we must achieve with wisdom and courage some fundamental reconstructions in our Christian thinking.

LECTURE II
THE NEED FOR RELIGION
I

One of the first effects of the idea of progress, whose development our last lecture traced, has been to increase immeasurably man's self reliance and to make him confident of humanity's power to take care of itself. At the heart of the idea of progress is man's new scientific control over life, and this new mastery, whereby the world seems ready to serve the purposes of those who will learn the laws, is the dominant influence in both the intellectual and practical activities of our age. That religion, in consequence, should seem to many of minor import, if not quite negligible, and that men, trusting themselves, their knowledge of law, their use of law-abiding forces, their power to produce change and to improve conditions, should find less need of trusting any one except themselves, was inevitable, but for all that it is fallacious. Already we have seen that a stumbling and uneven progress, precarious and easily frustrated, taking place upon a transient planet, goes but a little way to meet those elemental human needs with which religious faith has dealt. In our present lecture we propose a more specific consideration of this abiding necessity of religion in a progressive world.

How difficult it is to go back in imagination to the days before men grasped the meaning of natural law! We take gravitation for granted but, when Newton first proclaimed its law, the artillery of orthodox pulpits was leveled against him in angry consternation. Said one preacher, Newton "took from God that direct action on his works so constantly ascribed to him in Scripture and transferred it to material mechanism" and he "substituted gravitation for Providence." That preacher saw truly that the discovery of natural law was going to make a profound difference to religion. For ages men had been accustomed to look for the revelation of supernatural power in realms where they did not know the laws. And as men were tempted to look for the presence of God in realms where they did not know the laws, so in those realms they trusted God to do for them what they did not know how to do for themselves.

Then men began discovering natural laws, and every time they laid their hands on a new natural law they laid their hands on a new law-abiding force and began doing for themselves things of which their fathers had never dreamed. Stories of old-time miracles are overpassed in our modern days. Did Aladdin once rub a magic lamp and build a palace? To-day, knowledge of engineering laws enables us to achieve results that would put Aladdin quite to shame. He never dreamed a Woolworth Tower. Did the Israelites once cross the Red Sea dry-shod? One thing, however, they never would have hoped to do: to cross under and over the Hudson River day after day in multitudes, dry-shod. Did an axe-head float once when Elisha threw a stick into the water? But something no Elisha ever dreamed of seeing we see continually: iron ships navigating the ocean as though it were their natural element. Did Joshua once prolong the day for battle by the staying of the sun? Yet Joshua could never have conceived an habitual lighting of the city's homes and streets until by night they are more brilliant than by day. Did Jericho's walls once fall at the united shout of a besieging people? Those childlike besiegers, however, never dreamed of guns that could blast Jerichos to pieces from seventy miles away. Huxley was right when he said that our highly developed sciences have given us a command over the course of non-human nature greater than that once attributed to the magicians.

The consequence has been revolutionary. Old cries of dependence upon God grow unreal upon the lips of multitudes. Sometimes without knowing it, often without wanting it, men are drawn by the drift of modern thought away from all confidence in God and all consciousness of religious need. Consider two pictures. The first is an epidemic in New England in the seventeenth century. Everybody is thinking about God; the churches are full and days are passed in fasting and agonizing prayer. Only one way of getting rid of such an epidemic is known: men must gain new favour in the sight of God. The second picture is an epidemic in New England in the twentieth century. The churches are not full—they are closed by official order and popular consent to prevent the spread of germs. Comparatively few people are appealing to God; almost everybody is appealing to the health commissioner. Not many people are relying upon religion;

everybody is relying upon science. As one faces the pregnant significance of that contrast, one sees that in important sections of our modern life science has come to occupy the place that God used to have in the reliance of our forefathers. For the dominant fact of our generation is power over the world which has been put into our hands through the knowledge of laws, and the consequence is that the scientific mastery of life seems man's indispensable and sufficient resource.

The issue is not far to seek. Such has been public confidence in the efficacy and adequacy of this scientific control of life to meet all human needs, that in multitudes of minds religion has been crowded to the wall. Why should we trust God or concern ourselves with the deep secrets of religious faith, if all our need is met by learning laws, blowing upon our hands, and going to work? So even Christians come secretly to look upon their Christianity as a frill, something gracious but not indispensable, pleasant to live with but not impossible to live without. Christian preachers lose their ability, looking first upon their spiritual message and then upon their fellow men, to feel how desperately the two need each other. Religion has become an "elective in the university of life." But religion cannot persist as a frill; it either is central in its importance or else it is not true at all. Its great days come only when it is seen to be indispensable. We may use what artificial respiration we will upon the Church, the days of the Church's full power will not come until the conviction lays hold upon her that the endeavour to found civilization upon a materialistic science is leading us to perdition; that man needs desperately the ministry of religion, its insight into life's meanings, its control over life's use, its inward power for life's moral purposes; that man never needed this more than now, when the scientific control of life is arming him with so great ability to achieve his aims.

II

As we try to discern wherein man's need of religion lies with reference to the scientific control of life, let us start with the proposition that, when we have all the facts which science can discover, we still need a spiritual interpretation of the facts. All our experiences are made up of two elements: first, the outward circumstance, and second, the inward interpretation. On the one side is our environment, the world we live in, the things that befall us, the kaleidoscopic changes of fortune in the scenery of which our lives are set. On the other side are the inward interpretations that we give to this outward circumstance. Experience is compounded of these two elements.

This clearly is true in ordinary living. Two men, let us say, go to their physicians and are told that they have only a few months to live. This is the fact which faces both of them. As we watch them, however, we are at once aware that this fact is not the whole of their experience. One of the men crumples up; he "collapses into a yielding mass of plaintiveness and fear." Thinking of the event which he is facing, he sees nothing there but horror. That is his interpretation of it. The other man so looks upon the event which is coming that his family, far from having to support his spirit, are supported by him. He buoys them up; he carries them along; his faith and courage are contagious; and when he thinks of his death it appears in his eyes a great adventure concerning which the old hymn told the truth:

"It were a well-spent journey

Though seven deaths lay between."

That is his interpretation. As we regard the finished experiences of these two men, we see clearly that, while the same fact lay at the basis of both, it was the inward interpretation that determined the quality of the experience.

This power to transform facts so that they will be no longer merely facts, but facts plus an interpretation, is one of the most distinctive and significant elements in human life. The animals do not possess it. An event befalls a dog and, when the dog is through with it, the event is what it was before. The dog has done nothing to it. But the same event befalls a man and at once something begins to happen to it. It is clothed in the man's thought about it; it is dressed in his appreciation and understanding; it is transformed by his interpretations. The event comes out of that man's life something altogether different from what it was when it went in. The man can do almost anything with that event. For our experiences do not fall into our lives in single lumps, like meteors from a distant sky of fate; our experiences always are made up of the fortunes that befall us and the interpretations that we give to them.

So far as the relative importance of these two factors is concerned, we may see the truth in the application of our thought to happiness. If there is any area in human experience where the outward circumstance might be supposed to control the results, it is the realm of happiness; yet probably nine-tenths of the problem of happiness lies, not in the outward event, but in the inward interpretation. If we could describe those conditions in which the happiest people whom we have known have lived, can any one imagine the diversity of environment that would be represented in our accounts? Let them move in procession before the eyes of our imagination, those happy folk whose friendship has been the benediction of our lives! What a motley company they are! For some are blind, and some are crippled, and some are invalid; not many are rich and fortunate; many are poor—a company of handicapped but radiant spirits whose victorious lives, like the burning bush which Moses saw, have made in a desert a spot of holy ground. If, now, we ask why it is that happiness can be so amazingly independent of outward circumstance, this is the answer: every experience has two factors, the fortune that befalls and the inward interpretation of it; and, while we often cannot control the fortune, we always can help with the interpretation. That is in our power. That is the throne of our sovereignty over our lives.

III

The deep need of a worthy interpretation of life is just as urgent in a world where the idea of progress reigns as in any other, and to supply that need is one of the major functions of religion. For religion is something more than all the creeds that have endeavoured to express its thought. Religion is something more than all the organizations that have tried to incarnate its purposes. Religion is the human spirit, by the grace of God, seeking and finding an interpretation of experience that puts sense and worth, dignity, elevation, joy, and hope into life.

A body of students recently requested an address upon the subject: "What is the use of religion anyway?" The group of ideas behind the question is not hard to guess: that science gives us all the facts, that facts and their laws are all we need, that the scientific control of life guarantees progress, and that religion therefore is superfluous. But in such a statement one towering interrogation has been neglected: what about the interpretation of the very facts which science does present? Could not one address himself to the question of those students in some such way as this? You say that science has disclosed to us the leisureliness of the evolving universe. Come back, then, on the long road to the rear on which Bishop Usher's old date of creation is a way station an infinitesimal distance behind us; come back until together we stand at the universe's postern gate and look out into the mystery whence all things came, where no scientific investigation can ever go, where no one knows the facts. What do you make of it? Two voices rise in answer. One calls the world "a mechanical process, in which we may discover no aim or purpose whatever." And another voice says:

"The heavens declare the glory of God;

And the firmament showeth his handiwork."

That is not a difference in facts, upon which we can get our hands.

That is a difference in the interpretation of the facts.

Or come forward together to look into that mystery ahead, toward which this universe and we within it are so prodigiously plunging on. Do we not often feel, upon this earth whirling through space, like men and women who by some weird chance have found themselves upon a ship, ignorant of their point of departure and of their destination? For all the busyness with which we engage in many tasks, we cannot keep ourselves from slipping back at times to the ship's stern to look out along its wake and wonder whence we came, or from going at times also to its prow to wonder whither we are headed. What do you make of it? Toward what sort of haven is this good ship earth sailing—a port fortunate or ill? Or may it be there is no haven, only endless sailing on an endless sea by a ship that never will arrive? So questioning, we listen to conflicting voices. One says there is no future except ultimate annihilation, and another voice sings:

"All we have willed or hoped or dreamed

of good, shall exist."

That is not a difference in the facts, that eyes can see and hands handle; that is a difference in the interpretation of the facts.

Or from such large considerations come down into some familiar experience of daily life. Here is a man having a hard battle between right and wrong. There is no more impressive sight on earth to one who looks at it with understanding eyes. What do you make of this mysterious sense of duty which lays its magisterial hand upon us and will not be denied? At once various voices rise. Haeckel says the sense of duty is a "long series of phyletic modifications of the phronema of the cortex." That is his interpretation. And Wordsworth:

"Stern Daughter of the Voice of God!

O Duty!"

This sharp contrast is not a difference between facts, which can be pinned down as the Lilliputians pinned down Gulliver; it is a difference in the interpretation of the facts.

Or let us go together up some high hill from which we can look out upon the strange history of humankind. We see its agonies and wars, its rising empires followed by their ruinous collapse, and yet a mysterious advance, too, as though mankind, swinging up a spiral, met old questions upon a higher level, so that looking back to the Stone Age, for all the misery of this present time, we would be rather here than there. What can we make of it? Hauptmann's Michael Kramer says "All this life is the shuddering of a fever." And Paul says, "the eternal purpose which he purposed in Christ." That is not a difference in the facts. It is a difference in the interpretation of the facts.

Yet once more, come into the presence of death. The facts that human eyes can see are plain enough, but what can we make of it—this standing on the shore, waving farewell to a friendly ship that loses itself over the rim of the world? Says Thomson of the world's treatment of man,

"It grinds him some slow years of bitter breath,

Then grinds him back into eternal death."

And Paul says: "This corruptible must put on incorruption, and this mortal must put on immortality. But when this corruptible shall have put on incorruption, and this mortal shall have put on immortality, then shall come to pass the saying that is written, Death is swallowed up in victory." That is not a contrast between facts; that is a contrast between interpretations of facts.

Is it not plain why religion has such an unbreakable hold upon the human mind? The funeral of Christianity has been predicted many times but each time the deceased has proved too lively for the obsequies. In the middle of the eighteenth century they said that Christianity had one foot in the grave, but then came the amazing revival of religious life under the Wesleys. In the middle of the last century one wiseacre said, "In fifty years your Christianity will have died out"; yet, for all our failures, probably Christianity in all its history has never made more progress than in the last half century. If you ask why, one reason is clear: man cannot live in a universe of uninterpreted facts. The scientific approach to life is not enough. It does not cover all the ground. Men want to know what life spiritually means and they want to know that it "means intensely, and means good." Facts alone are like pieces of irritating grit that get into the oyster shell; the pearl of life is created by the interpretations which the facts educe.

In this difference between the facts of experience and their interpretations lies the secret of the contrast between our two words existence and life. Even before we define the difference, we feel it. To exist is one thing; to live is another. Existence is comprised of the bare facts of life alone—the universe in which we live, our heritage and birth, our desires and their satisfactions, growth, age and death. All the facts that science can display before us comprise existence. But life is something more. Life is existence clothed in spiritual meanings; existence seen with a worthy purpose at the heart of it and hope ahead, existence informed by the spirit's insights and understandings, transfigured and glorified by the spirit's faiths and hopes. It follows, therefore, that while existence is given us to start with, life is a spiritual achievement. A man must take the facts of his existence whether he wants to or not, but he makes his life by the activity of his soul. The facts of existence are like so much loose type, which can be set up to many meanings. One man leaves those facts in chaotic disarrangement or sets them up into cynical affirmations, and he exists. But another man takes the same facts and by spiritual insight makes them mean gloriously, and he lives indeed. To suppose that mankind ever can be satisfied with existence only and can be called off from the endeavour to achieve this more abundant life, is utterly to misconceive the basic facts of human nature. And this profound need for a spiritual interpretation of life is not satisfied by an idea of temporal progress, stimulated by a few circumstances which predispose our minds to immediate expectancy.

IV

When, therefore, any one asserts the adequacy of the scientific approach to life, one answer stands ready to our hand: science deals primarily with facts and their laws, not with their spiritual interpretations. To put the same truth in another way, science deals with one specially abstracted aspect of the facts; it drains them of their qualitative elements and, reducing them to their quantitative elements, it proceeds to weigh and measure them and state their laws. It moves in the realm of actualities and not in the realm of values. One science, for example, takes a gorgeous sunset and reduces it to the constituent ether waves that cause the colour. What it says about the sunset is true, but it is not the whole truth. Ask anybody who has ever seen the sun riding like a golden galleon down the western sea! Another science takes a boy and reduces him to his Bertillon measurements and at the top of the statistics writes his name, "John Smith." That is the truth about John Smith, but it is not the whole truth. Ask his mother and see! Another science takes our varied and vibrant mental life and reduces it to its physical basis and states its laws. That is the truth about our mental life, but it is not the whole truth. What is more, it is not that part of the truth by which men really live. For men live by love and joy and hope and faith and spiritual insight. When these things vanish life is

"a tale Told by an idiot, full of sound and fury, Signifying nothing."

When a man takes that quantitative aspect of reality, which is the special province of natural science, as though it were the whole of reality, he finds himself in a world where the physical forces are in control. We, ourselves, according to this aspect of life, are the product of physical forces — marionettes, dancing awhile because physical forces are pulling on the strings. In a word, when a man takes that quantitative aspect of reality, which natural science presents, as though it were the whole of reality, he becomes a materialistic fatalist, and on that basis we cannot permanently build either personal character or a stable civilization. It is not difficult, then, to see one vital significance of Jesus Christ: he has given us the most glorious interpretation of life's meaning that the sons of men have ever had. The fatherhood of God, the friendship of the Spirit, the sovereignty of righteousness, the law of love, the glory of service, the coming of the Kingdom, the eternal hope — there never was an interpretation of life to compare with that. If life often looks as though his interpretation were too good to be true, we need not be surprised. Few things in the universe are as superficially they look. The earth looks flat and, as long as we gaze on it, it never will look any other way, but it is spherical for all that. The earth looks stationary and if we live to be as old as Methuselah we never will see it move, but it is moving — seventy-five times faster than a cannon ball! The sun looks as though it rose in the east and set in the west, and we never can make it look any other way, but it does not rise nor set at all. So far as this earth is concerned, the sun is standing still enough. We look as though we walked with our heads up and our feet down, and we never can make ourselves look otherwise, but someone finding a safe stance outside this whirling sphere would see us half the time walking with our heads down and our feet up. Few things are ever the way they look, and the end of all scientific research, as of all spiritual insight, is to get behind the way things look to the way things are. Walter Pater has a rememberable phrase, "the hiddenness of perfect things." One meaning, therefore, which Christ has for Christians lies in the realm of spiritual interpretation. He has done for us there what Copernicus and Galileo did in astronomy: he has moved us out from our flat earth into his meaningful universe, full of moral worth and hope. He has become to us in this, our inner need, what the luminous phrase of the Book of Job describes, "An interpreter, one among a thousand." And in spite of all our immediate expectancy, born out of our scientific control of life, mankind never needed that service more than now.

V

There is a second proposition to which we should attend as we endeavour to define the need for religion with reference to the scientific mastery of life. Consider why so often men are tempted to suppose that science is adequate for human purposes. Is it not because science supplies men with power? Steam, electricity, petroleum, radium—with what progressive mastery over the latent resources of the universe does science move from one area of energy to another, until in the imagination of recent generations she has seemed to stand saying: all power is given unto me in heaven and in earth. With such power to bestow, is she not our rightful mistress? But who that has walked with discerning eyes through these last few years can any longer be beguiled by that fallacious vision? Look at what we are doing with this new power that science has given us! The business to which steel and steam and electricity, explosives and poisons have recently been put does not indicate that humanity's problem is solved when new power is put into our hands. Even the power of wide-spread communication can so be used that a war which began in Serajevo will end with lads from Kamchatka and Bombay blasted to pieces by the same shell on a French battlefield. Even the power of modern finance can be so used that nations will exhaust the credit of generations yet unborn in waging war. How some folk keep their cheap and easy optimism about humanity's use of its new energies is a mystery. We have come pretty near to ruining ourselves with them already. If we do not achieve more spiritual control over them than we have yet exhibited we will ruin ourselves with them altogether. Once more in history a whole civilization will commit suicide like Saul falling on his own sword.

The scientific control of life, by itself, creates more problems than it solves. The problem of international disarmament, for example, has been forced on us by the fear of that perdition to the suburbs of which our race has manifestly come through the misuse of scientific knowledge. Humanity is disturbed about itself because it has discovered that it is in possession of power enough to wreck the world. Never before did mankind have so much energy to handle. Multitudes of people, dubious as to whether disarmament is practical, are driven like shuttles back and forth between that doubt, upon the one side, and the certainty, upon the other, that armament is even less practical. The statisticians have been at work upon this last war and their figures, like the measurements of the astronomers, grow to a size so colossal that the tentacles of our imaginations slip off them when we try to grasp their size. The direct costs of this last war, which left us with more and harder difficulties than we had at the beginning, were about $186,000,000,000. Is that practical? At the beginning of 1922 almost all the nations in Europe, although by taxation they were breaking their people's financial backs, were spending far more than their income, and in the United States, far and away the richest nation on the planet, we faced an enormous deficit. Is that practical? In this situation, with millions of people unemployed, with starvation rampant, with social revolution stirring in every country—not because people are bad, not because they impatiently love violence, but because they cannot stand forever the social strain and economic consequence of war—what were we doing? We were launching battleships which cost $42,000,000 to build, which cost $2,000,000 a year to maintain and which, in a few years, would be towed out to sea to be used as an experimental target to try out some new armour-piercing shell. I wonder if our children's children will look back on that spectacle and call it practical. In 1912 the naval expenses of this country were about $136,000,000. In 1921 our naval expenses were about $641,000,000—approximately five times greater in nine years. So over all the earth war preparations were pyramiding with an ever accelerating momentum. And because any man can see that we must stop sometime, we have been trying desperately to stop now; to turn our backs upon this mad endeavour to build civilization upon a materialistic basis, bulwarked by physical force; to turn our faces toward spiritual forces, fair play, reasonable conference, good-will, service and co-operation.

Yet how hard it is to make the change effective! Long ages ago in the primeval jungle, the dogs' ancestors used to turn around three times in the thicket before they lay down, that they might make a comfortable spot to nestle in, and now your highbred Pekingese will turn around three times upon his silken cushion although there is no earthly reason why he should. So difficult is it to breed beasts and men out of their inveterate habits. So hard is it going to be to make men give up the idea that force is a secure foundation for international relationships. Yet somehow that change must be made. They are having trouble with the housing problem in Tokyo and the reason is simple. Tokyo is built on earthquake ground and it is insecure. You cannot put great houses on unstable foundations. One story, two stories, three stories—that is about as high as they dare go. But in New York City one sees the skyscrapers reaching up their sixty stories into the air. The explanation is not difficult: Manhattan Island is solid rock. If you are going to build great structures you must have great foundations. And civilization is a vast and complicated structure. We cannot build it on physical force. That is too shaky. We must build it upon spiritual foundations.

There are those who suppose that this can be done by progress through the scientific control of life, and who treat religion as a negligible element. Such folk forget that while a cat will lap her milk contentedly from a saucer made of Wedgwood or china, porcelain or earthenware, and will feel no curiosity about the nature of the receptacle from which she drinks, human beings are not animals who thus can take their food and ask no questions about the universe in which it is served to them. We want to know about life's origin and meaning and destiny. We cannot keep our questions at home. We cannot stop thinking. If this universe is fundamentally physical, if the only spark of spiritual life which it ever knew is the fitful flame of our own unsteady souls, if it came from dust and to dust will return, leaving behind no recollection of the human labour, sacrifice and aspiration which for a little time it unconsciously enshrined, that outlook makes an incalculable difference to our present lives. For then our very minds themselves, which have developed here by accident upon this wandering island in the skies, represent the only kind of mind there is, and what we do not know never was thought about or cared for or purposed by anyone, and we, alone in knowing, are ourselves unknown.

The consequence of this sort of thinking, which is the essence of irreligion, is to be seen on every side of us in folk who, having thus lost all confidence in God and the reality of the spiritual world, still try to labour for the good of men. They have kept one part of Christianity, its ideals of character and service; they have lost the other part, which assures them about God. In a word, they are trying to build an idealistic and serviceable life upon a godless basis. Now, the difficulty with this attitude toward life lies here: it demands a quality of spirit for which it cannot supply the motive. It demands social hope, confidence, enthusiasm and sacrifice, and all the while it cuts their nerves. It tells men that the universe is fundamentally a moral desert, that it never was intended even to have an oasis of civilization in it, that if we make one grow it will be by dint of our own effort against the deadset of the universe's apathy, that if, by our toil, an oasis is achieved, it will have precarious tenure in such alien and inhospitable soil, and that in the end it will disappear before the onslaught of the cosmic forces; yet in the same breath it tells men to work for that oasis with hope, confidence, joy and enthusiastic sacrifice. This is a world view which asks of men a valorous and expensive service for which it cannot supply the driving power. Yet many of our universities are presenting just that outlook upon life to our young men and women. The youth are being urged to fight courageously and sacrificially for righteousness upon the earth, and at the same time they are presented with a view of the background and destiny of human life similar to that which Schopenhauer expressed: "Truly optimism cuts so sorry a figure in this theatre of sin, suffering, and death that we should have to regard it as a piece of sarcasm, if Hume had not explained its origin—insincere flattery of God in the arrogant expectation of gain."

What this generation, which so disparages religion and like the ancient Sadducee calls its good right arm its god, will ultimately discover is that the fight for righteousness in character and in society is a long and arduous campaign. The Bible says that a thousand years in God's sight are but as yesterday when it is past, and as a watch in the night. It certainly seems that way. It is a long and roundabout journey to the Promised Land. Generations die and fall by the way. The road is white with the bones of pilgrims who attained not the promises but saw them and greeted them from afar. Some Giordano Bruno, who gives himself to the achievement of mankind's high aims, is burned at the stake; centuries pass and on the very spot where he was martyred a monument is built with this inscription on it: "Raised to Giordano Bruno by the generation which he foresaw." This is exhilarating when the story is finished, but in the meantime it is hard work being Giordano Bruno and sacrificially labouring for a cause which you care enough for and believe enough in and are sure enough about so that you will die for it. When such faith and hope and sacrifice are demanded one cannot get them by exhortation, by waving a wand of words to conjure his enthusiasm up. Nothing will do but a world-view adequate to supply motives for the service it demands. Nothing will do but religion.

One wonders why the preachers do not feel this more and so recover their consciousness of an indispensable mission. One wonders that the churches can be so timid and dull and negative, that our sermons can be so pallid and inconsequential. One wonders why in the pulpit we have so many flutes and so few trumpets. For here is a world with the accumulating energies of the new science in its hands, living in the purlieus of hell because it cannot gain spiritual mastery over the very power in which it glories. Here is a world which must build its civilization on spiritual bases or else collapse into abysmal ruin and which cannot achieve the task though all the motives of self-preservation cry out to have it done, because men lack the very elements of faith and character which it is the business of religion to supply.

VI

We have said that when science has given us all its facts we still need a spiritual interpretation of the facts; that when science has put all its energies into our hands we still need spiritual mastery over their use. Let us say in conclusion that, when science has given us all its power, we still need another kind of power which it is not the business of science to supply. Long ago somebody who knew the inner meaning of religion wrote:

"The Lord is my shepherd; I shall not want.

He maketh me to lie down in green pastures;

He leadeth me beside still waters.

He restoreth my soul."

That last phrase sums up one of the deepest needs of human life. We are in constant want of spiritual repair; we are lost without a fresh influx of inward power; we desperately need to have our souls restored. A young British soldier once came in from the trenches where his aggressive powers had been in full employ and, having heard one of the finest concert companies that London could send out, he wrote in a letter to his family: "I have just come down from the trenches, and have been listening to one of the best concerts I ever attended. It makes one feel that perhaps there is a good God after all." The two aspects of life which that soldier discovered in himself all men possess. One takes us to life's trenches; the other throws us back on some revelation of grace and beauty that we may be sure of God. With one we seek aggressively to master life; with the other we seek receptively to be inspired. Every normal man needs these two kinds of influence: one to send him informed and alert to his tasks, the other to float his soul off its sandbars on the rising tide of spiritual reassurance and power. Every normal man needs two attitudes: one when he goes into action determined to do his work and to do it well, and the other when he subdues his spirit to receptivity and with the Psalmist cries,

"My soul, wait thou in silence for God only;

For my expectation is from him."

When science has given us all the power it can, we still need another kind of power which science cannot give.

Whatever else the scientific control of life may have accomplished, it has not saved mankind from the old and devastating problems of trouble and sin. So far as individual experience of these is concerned, there is little discernable difference between two thousand years before Christ and two thousand years afterward. Still disasters fall upon our lives, sometimes as swift in their assault as wild beasts leaping from an unsuspected ambush. Still troubles come, long drawn out and wearying, like the monotonous dripping of water with which old torturers used to drive their victims mad. Still sins bring shame to the conscience and tragic consequence to the life, and tiresome work, losing the buoyancy of its first inspiration, drags itself out into purposeless effort and bores us with its futility. Folk now, as much as ever in all history, need to have their souls restored. The scientific control of life, however, is not adequate for that. Electricity and subways and motor cars do not restore the soul; and to know that there are millions upon millions of solar systems, like our own, scattered through space does not restore the soul; and to delve in the sea or to fly in the air or to fling our words through the ether does not restore the soul. The need of religion is perennial and would be though our scientific control over life were extended infinitely beyond our present hope, for the innermost ministry of religion to human life is the restoration of the soul.

In this fact lies the failure of that type of naturalism which endeavours to keep religion as a subjective experience and denies the reality of an objective God. If we are not already familiar with this attempted substitution we soon shall be, for our young people are being taught it in many a classroom now. One of the basic principles of this new teaching is belief in the spiritual life but, when one inquires where the spiritual life is, he discovers that it is altogether within ourselves—there is no original, creative and abiding Spiritual Life from whom we come, by whom we are sustained, in whom we live. Rather, as flowers reveal in their fragrance a beauty which is not in the earth where they grow nor in the roots on which they depend, so our spiritual life is the mysterious refinement of the material out of which we are constructed, and it has nothing to correspond with it in the source from which we sprang. Nevertheless, the new naturalism exalts this spiritual life within us, calls it our crown and glory, bids us cultivate and diffuse it, says about it nearly everything a Christian says except that it is a revelation of eternal reality. Moreover, it is difficult to differentiate from this outspoken group of professed naturalists another group of humanists who do retain the idea of God, but merely as the sum total of man's idealistic life. "God," says one exponent, "is the farthest outreach of our human ideals." That is to say, our spiritual lives created God, not God our spiritual lives. God, as one enthusiastic devotee of this new cult has put it, is a sort of Uncle Sam, the pooling of the idealistic imaginations of multitudes. Of course he does not exist, yet in a sense he is real; he is the projection of our loyalties, affections, hopes.

It should go without saying that this idea of God has about as much intellectual validity as belief in Santa Claus and is even more sentimental, in that it is a deliberate attempt to disguise in pleasant and familiar terms a fundamentally materialistic interpretation of reality. The vital failure of this spiritualized naturalism, however, lies in the inability of its Uncle Sam to meet the deepest needs on account of which men at their best have been religious. This deified projection of our ideals we made up ourselves and so we cannot really pray to him; he does not objectively exist and so has no unifying meaning which puts purposefulness into creation and hope ahead of it; he does not care for any one or anything and so we may not trust him; and neither in sin can he forgive, cleanse, restore, empower, nor in sorrow comfort and sustain. A god who functions so poorly is not much of a god. Once more, therefore, one wonders why in a generation when, not less, but more, because of all our scientific mastery the souls of men are starved and tired, the Church is not captured by a new sense of mission. It is precisely in a day when the active and pugnacious energies of men are most involved in the conquest of the world that the spirit becomes most worn for lack of sustenance. To be assured of the nearness and reality and availability of the spiritual world is a matter of life and death to multitudes of folk to-day. There could hardly be a more alluring time in which to make the Holy Spirit real to the world. For the supreme moral asset in any man's life is not his aggressiveness nor his pugnacity, but his capacity to be inspired—to be inspired by great books, great music, by love and friendship; to be inspired by great faiths, great hopes, great ideals; to be inspired supremely by the Spirit of God. For so we are lifted until the things we tried to see and could not we now can see because of the altitude at which we stand, and the things we tried to do and could not we now can do because of the fellowship in which we live. To one asserting the adequacy of the scientific control of life, therefore, the Christian's third answer is clear: man's deepest need is spiritual power, and spiritual power comes out of the soul's deep fellowships with the living God.

Such, then, is the abiding need of religion in a scientific age. To be scientifically minded is one of the supreme achievements of mankind. To love truth, as science loves it, to seek truth tirelessly, as science seeks it, to reveal the latent resources of the universe in hope that men will use them for good and not for evil, as science does, is one of the chief glories of our race. When, however, we have taken everything that science gives, it is not enough for life. When we have facts, we still need a spiritual interpretation of facts; when we have all the scientific forces that we can get our hands upon, we still need spiritual mastery over their use; and, beyond all the power that science gives, we need that inward power which comes from spiritual fellowships alone. Religion is indispensable. To build human life upon another basis is to erect civilization upon sand, where the rain descends and the floods come and the winds blow and beat upon the house and it falls and great is the fall thereof.

LECTURE III
THE GOSPEL AND SOCIAL PROGRESS
I

Our last lecture started with the proposition that the dominant influence in the intellectual and practical activity of the modern age is man's scientific mastery over life. This present lecture considers one of the consequences of this primary fact: namely, the humanitarian desire to take advantage of this scientific control of life so to change social conditions that mankind may be relieved from crushing handicaps which now oppress it. For the growth of scientific knowledge and control has been coincident with a growth of humanitarian sentiment. This movement for human relief and social reform, in the midst of which we live, is one of the chief influences of our time. It has claimed the allegiance of many of the noblest folk among us. Its idealism, its call to sacrifice, the concreteness of the tasks which it undertakes and of the gains which it achieves, have attracted alike the fine spirits and the practical abilities of our generation. What attitude shall the Christian Church take toward this challenging endeavour to save society? How shall she regard this passionate belief in the possibility of social betterment and this enthusiastic determination to achieve it? The question is one of crucial importance and the Church is far from united on its answer. Some Christians claim the whole movement as the child of the Church, born of her spirit and expressing her central purpose; others disclaim the whole movement as evil and teach that the world must grow increasingly worse until some divine cataclysm shall bring its hopeless corruption to an end; others treat the movement as useful but of minor import, while they try to save men by belief in dogmatic creeds or by carefully engineered emotional experiences. Meanwhile, no words can exaggerate the fidelity, the vigour, the hopefulness, and the elevated spirit with which many of our best young men and women throw themselves into this campaign for better conditions of living. Surely, the intelligent portion of the Church would better think as clearly as possible about a matter of such crucial import.

At first sight, the devotee of social Christianity is inclined impatiently to brush aside as mere ignorant bigotry on the Church's part all cautious suspicion of the social movement. But there is one real difficulty which the thoughtful Christian must perceive when he compares the characteristic approach to the human problem made by the social campaign, on the one side, and by religion, on the other. Much of the modern social movement seems to proceed upon the supposition that we can save mankind by the manipulation of outward circumstance. There are societies to change everything that can be changed and, because the most obvious and easy subjects of transformation are the external arrangements of human life, men set themselves first and chiefly to change those. We are always trying to improve the play by shifting the scenery. But no person of insight ever believed that the manipulation of circumstance alone can solve man's problems. Said Emerson, "No change of circumstances can repair a defect of character." Said Herbert Spencer, "No philosopher's stone of a constitution can produce golden conduct from leaden instincts." Said James Anthony Froude, "Human improvement is from within outwards." Said Carlyle, "Fool! the Ideal is in thyself, the impediment too is in thyself: thy Condition is but the stuff thou art to shape that same Ideal out of." Said Mrs. Browning:

"It takes a soul,

To move a body: it takes a high-souled man

To move the masses even to a cleaner stye:

….. Ah, your Fouriers failed,

Because not poets enough to understand

That life develops from within."

Now, religion's characteristic approach to the human problem is represented by this conviction that "life develops from within." So far from expecting to save mankind by the manipulation of outward circumstance, it habitually has treated outward circumstance as of inferior moment in comparison with the inner attitudes and resources of the spirit. Economic affluence, for example, has not seemed to Christianity in any of its historic forms indispensable to man's well-being; rather, economic affluence has been regarded as a danger to be escaped or else to be resolutely handled as one would handle fire — useful if well managed but desperately perilous if uncontrolled. Nor can it be said that Christianity has consistently maintained this attitude without having in actual experience much ground for holding it. The possession of economic comfort has never yet guaranteed a decent life, much less a spiritually satisfactory one. The morals of Fifth Avenue are not such that it can look down on Third Avenue, nor is it possible anywhere to discern gradation of character on the basis of relative economic standing. It is undoubtedly true that folks and families often have their moral stamina weakened and their personalities debauched by sinking into discouraging poverty, but it is an open question whether more folks and families have not lost their souls by rising into wealth. Still, after all these centuries, the "rich fool," with his overflowing barns and his soul that sought to feed itself on corn, is a familiar figure; still it is as easy for a camel to go through a needle's eye as for a rich man to enter the Kingdom of Heaven. When, therefore, the Christian, approaching the human problem, not from without in, but from within out, runs upon this modern social movement endeavouring to save mankind by the manipulation of outward circumstance, his cautious and qualified consent may be neither so ignorant nor so unreasonable as it at first appears.

As an example of manipulated circumstance in which we are asked to trust, consider the new international arrangements upon which the world leans so heavily for its hopes of peace. Surely, he would be a poor Christian who did not rejoice in every reasonable expectation which new forms of co-operative organization can fulfil. But he would be a thoughtless Christian, too, if he did not see that all good forms of international organization are trellises to give the vines of human relationship a fairer chance to grow; but if the vines themselves maintain their old acid quality, bringing out of their own inward nature from roots of bitterness grapes that set the people's teeth on edge, then no external trellises will solve the problem. It is this Christian approach to life, from within out, which causes the common misunderstanding between the social movement and the Church. The first thinks mainly of the importance of the trellis; the second thinks chiefly about the quality of the vine.

The more deep and transforming a man's own religious experience has been, the more he will insist upon the importance of this inward approach. Here is a man who has had a profound evangelical experience. He has gone down into the valley of the shadow with a deep sense of spiritual need; he has found in Christ a Saviour who has lifted him up into spiritual freedom and victory; he has gone out to live with a sense of unpayable indebtedness to him. He has had, in a word, a typical religious experience at its best with three elements at the heart of it: a great need, a great salvation, a great gratitude. When such a man considers the modern social movement, however beautiful its spirit or admirable its concrete gains, it seems to him superficial if it presents itself as a panacea. It does not go deep enough to reach the soul's real problems. The continual misunderstanding between the Church and the social movement has, then, this explanation: the characteristic approach of the Christian Gospel to the human problem is from within out; the characteristic approach of much of the modern social movement is from without in.

II

If, therefore, the Christian Gospel is going to be true to itself, it must carefully preserve amid the pressure of our modern social enthusiasms certain fundamental emphases which are characteristic of its genius. It must stress the possibility and the necessity of the inward transformation of the lives of men. We know now that a thorny cactus does not have to stay a thorny cactus; Burbank can change it. We know that a crab-apple tree does not have to stay a crab-apple tree; it can be grafted and become an astrakhan. We know that a malarial swamp does not have to stay a malarial swamp; it can be drained and become a health resort. We know that a desert does not have to stay a desert; it can be irrigated and become a garden. But while all these possibilities of transformation are opening up in the world outside of us, the most important in the series concerns the world within us. The primary question is whether human nature is thus transformable, so that men can be turned about, hating what formerly they loved and loving what once they hated. Said Tolstoy, whose early life had been confessedly vile: "Five years ago faith came to me; I believed in the doctrine of Jesus, and my whole life underwent a sudden transformation. What I had once wished for I wished for no longer, and I began to desire what I had never desired before. What had once appeared to me right now became wrong, and the wrong of the past I beheld as right."

So indispensable to the welfare of the world is this experience, that we Christians need to break loose from our too narrow conceptions of it and to set it in a large horizon. We have been too often tempted to make of conversion a routine emotional experience. Even Jonathan Edwards was worried about himself in this regard. He wrote once in his diary: "The chief thing that now makes me in any measure question my good estate is my not having experienced conversion in those particular steps wherein the people of New England, and anciently the dissenters of old England, used to experience it." Poor Jonathan! How many have been so distraught! But the supreme folly of any man's spiritual life is to try thus to run himself into the mold of any other man's experience. There is no regular routine in spiritual transformation. Some men come in on a high tide of feeling, like Billy Bray, the drunken miner, who, released from his debasing slavery and reborn into a vigorous life, cried, "If they were to put me into a barrel I would shout glory out through the bunghole! Praise the Lord!" Some men come in like Bushnell, the New England scholar and preacher, who, when he was an unbelieving tutor at Yale, fell on his knees in the quiet of his study and said, "O God, I believe there is an eternal difference between right and wrong and I hereby give myself up to do the right and to refrain from the wrong." Some men break up into the new life suddenly like the Oxford graduate who, having lived a dissolute life until six years after his graduation from the university in 1880, picked up in his room one day Drummond's "Natural Law in the Spiritual World," and, lo! the light broke suddenly — "I rejoiced there and then in a conversion so astounding that the whole village heard of it in less than twenty-four hours." Some come slowly, like old John Livingstone, who said, "I do not remember any particular time of conversion, or that I was much cast down or lift up." Spiritual transformation is infinitely various because it is so infinitely vital;

but behind all the special forms of experience stands the colossal fact that men can be transformed by the Spirit of God.

That this experience of inward enlightenment and transformation should ever be neglected or minimized or forgotten or crowded out is the more strange because one keeps running on it outside religion as well as within. John Keats, when eighteen years old, was handed one day a copy of Spenser's poems. He never had known before what his life was meant to be. He found out that day. Like a voice from heaven his call came in the stately measures of Spenser's glorious verse. He knew that he was meant to be a poet. Upon this master fact that men can be inwardly transformed Christ laid his hand and put it at the very center of his gospel. All through the New Testament there is a throb of joy which, traced back, brings one to the assurance that no man need stay the way he is. Among the gladdest, solemnest words in the records of our race are such passages in the New Testament as this: Fornicators, adulterers, thieves, covetous, drunkards, revelers, extortioners, such were some of you; but ye were washed, but ye were sanctified, but ye were justified in the name of the Lord Jesus Christ and in the Spirit of our God. One cannot find in the New Testament anything stiff and stilted about this experience. Paul's change came suddenly; Peter's came slowly. They did not even have, as we have come to have, a settled word to describe the experience. Ask James what it is and, practical-minded man that he is, he calls it conversion—being turned around. Ask Peter what it is and, as he looks back upon his old benighted condition, he cries that it is like coming out of the darkness into a marvelous light. Ask Paul what it is and, with his love of superlative figures, he cries that it is like being dead and being raised again with a great resurrection. Ask John what it is and, with his mystical spirit, he says that it is being born again. See the variety that comes from vitality—no stiff methods, no stiff routine of experience, but throbbing through the whole book the good news of an illuminating, liberating, transforming experience that can make men new!

It is the more strange that this central element in the Christian Gospel should be neglected in the interests of social reformation because it is so indispensable to social reformation. Wherever a new social hope allures the efforts of forward-looking men, there is one argument against the hope which always rises. You cannot do that—men say—human nature is against it; human nature has always acted another way; you cannot change human nature; your hope is folly. As one listens to such skepticism he sees that men mean by human nature a static, unalterable thing, huge, inert, changeless, a dull mass that resists all transformation. The very man who says that may be an engineer. He may be speaking in the next breath with high enthusiasm about a desert in Arizona where they are bringing down the water from the hills and where in a few years there will be no desert, but orange groves stretching as far as the eye can reach, and eucalyptus trees making long avenues of shade, and roses running wild, as plenteous as goldenrod in a New England field. But while about physical nature he is as hopeful of possible change as a prophet, for human nature he thinks nothing can be done.

From the Christian point of view this idea of human nature is utterly false. So far from being stiff and set, human nature is the most plastic, the most changeable thing with which we deal. It can be brutalized beneath the brutes; it can rise into companionship with angels. Our primitive forefathers, as our fairy tales still reveal, believed that men and women could be changed into anything—into trees, rocks, wolves, bears, kings and fairy sprites. One of the most prominent professors of sociology in America recently said that these stories are a poetic portraiture of something which eternally is true. Men can be transformed. That is a basic fact, and it is one of the central emphases of the Christian Gospel. Of all days in which that emphasis should be remembered, the chiefest is the day when men are thinking about social reformation.

III

It is only a clear recognition of the crucial importance of man's inward transformation which can prepare us for a proper appreciation of the social movement's meaning. For one point of contact between religion's approach to the human problem from within out and reformation's approach from without in lies here: to change social environments which oppress and dwarf and defile the lives of men is one way of giving the transforming Spirit a fair chance to reach and redeem them. All too slowly does the truth lay hold upon the Church that our very personalities themselves are social products, that we are born out of society and live in it and are molded by it, that without society we should not be human at all, and that the influences which play upon our lives, whether redeeming or degrading, are socially mediated. A man who says that he believes in the ineffable value of human personalities and who professes to desire their transformation and yet who has no desire to give them better homes, better cities, better family relationships, better health, better economic resources, better recreations, better books and better schools, is either an ignoramus who does not see what these things mean in the growth of souls, or else an unconscious hypocrite who does not really care so much about the souls of men as he says he does.

An illuminating illustration of this fact is to be seen in the expanding ideals of missionary work. When the missionaries first went to the ends of the earth they went to save souls one by one. They went out generally with a distinctly, often narrowly, individualistic motive. They were trying to gather into the ark a few redeemed spirits out of the wreck of a perishing world; they were not thinking primarily of building a kingdom of social righteousness in the earth. Consider, then, the fascinating story of the way the missionaries, whatever may have been the motives with which they started, have become social reformers. If the missionaries were to take the Gospel to the people, they had to get to the people. So they became the explorers of the world. It was the missionaries who opened up Asia and Africa. Was there ever a more stirring story of adventure than is given us in the life of David Livingstone? Then when the missionaries had reached the people to give them the Gospel, they had to give them the Bible. So they became the philologists and translators of the world. They built the lexicons and grammars. They translated the Bible into more than a hundred languages on the continent of Africa alone. Carey and his followers did the same for over a score of languages in India. The Bible to-day is available in over six hundred living languages. Everywhere this prodigious literary labour has been breaking down the barriers of speech and thought between the peoples. If ever we do get a decent internationalism, how much of it will rest back upon this pioneer spade work of the missionaries, digging through the barricades of language that separate the minds of men! When, then, the missionaries had books to give the people, the people had to learn to read. So the missionaries became educators, and wherever you find the church you find the school. But what is the use of educating people who do not understand how to be sanitary, who live in filth and disease and die needlessly, and how can you take away old superstitions and not put new science in their places, or deprive the people of witch doctors without offering them substitutes? So the missionaries became physicians, and one of the most beneficent enterprises that history records is medical missions. What is the use, however, of helping people to get well when their economic condition is such, their standards of life so low, that they continue to fall sick again in spite of you? So the missionaries are becoming industrial reformers, agriculturalists, chemists, physicists, engineers, rebuilding wherever they can the economic life and comfort of their people. The missionary cause itself has been compelled, whether it would or not, to grow socially-minded. As Dan Crawford says about the work in Africa: "Here, then, is Africa's challenge to its Missionaries. Will they allow a whole continent to live like beasts in such hovels, millions of negroes cribbed, cabined, and confined in dens of disease? No doubt it is our diurnal duty to preach that the soul of all improvement is the improvement of the soul. But God's equilateral triangle of body, soul, and spirit must never be ignored. Is not the body wholly ensouled, and is not the soul wholly embodied? . . . In other words, in Africa the only true fulfilling of your heavenly calling is the doing of earthly things in a heavenly manner."

Indeed, if any one is tempted to espouse a narrowly individualistic gospel of regeneration, let him go to the Far East and take note of Buddhism. Buddhism in wide areas of its life is doing precisely what the individualists recommend. It is a religion of personal comfort and redemption. It is not mastered by a vigorous hope of social reformation. In many ways it is extraordinarily like medieval Christianity. Consider this definition of his religion that was given by one Buddhist teacher: "Religion," he said, "is a device to bring peace of mind in the midst of conditions as they are." Conditions as they are—settle down in them; be comfortable about them; do not try to change them; let no prayer for the Kingdom of God on earth disturb them; and there seek for yourselves "peace of mind in the midst of conditions as they are." And the Buddhist teacher added, "My religion is pure religion." But is there any such thing as really caring about the souls of men and not caring about social habits, moral conditions, popular recreations, economic handicaps that in every way affect them? Of all deplorable and degenerate conceptions of religion can anything be worse than to think of it as a "device to bring peace of mind in the midst of conditions as they are?" Yet one finds plenty of Church members in America whose idea of the "simple Gospel" comes perilously near that Buddhist's idea of "pure religion."

The utter futility of endeavouring to care about the inward transformation of men's lives while not caring about their social environment is evident when one thinks of our international relationships and their recurrent issue in war. War surely cannot be thought of any longer as a school for virtue. We used to think it was. We half believed the German war party when they told us about the disciplinary value of their gigantic establishment, and when Lord Roberts assured us that war was tonic for the souls of peoples we were inclined to think that he was right. When, in answer to our nation's call, our men went out to fight and all our people were bound up in a fellowship of devotion to a common cause, so stimulated were we that we almost were convinced that out of such an experience there might come a renaissance of spiritual quality and life. Is there anybody who can blind his eyes to the facts now? Every competent witness in Europe and America has had to say that we are on a far lower moral level than we were before the war. Crimes of sex, crimes of violence, have been unprecedented. Large areas of Europe are to-day in a chaos so complete that not one man in a thousand in America even dimly imagines it, with a break-down of all the normal, sustaining relationships and privileges of civilized life, and with an accompanying collapse of character unprecedented in Christendom since the days of the Black Plague. If we are wise we will never again go down into hell expecting to come up with spirits redeemed.

To be sure, there are many individuals of such moral stamina that they have come out of this experience personally the better, not the worse. There are people who would build into the fiber of their character any experience that earth could offer them. But if we are thinking of the moral stability and progress of mankind, surely there is nothing in the processes of war, as we have seen them, or the results of war, as they now lie about us, that would lead us to trust to them for help. War takes a splendid youth willing to serve the will of God in his generation before he falls on sleep and teaches him the skilful trick of twisting a bayonet into the abdomen of an enemy. War takes a loyal-spirited man who is not afraid of anything under heaven and teaches him to drop bombs on undefended towns, to kill perchance the baby suckled at her mother's breast. The father of one of our young men, back from France, finding that his son, like many others, would not talk, rebuked him for his silence. "Just one thing I will tell you," the son answered. "One night I was on patrol in No Man's Land, and suddenly I came face to face with a German about my own age. It was a question of his life or mine. We fought like wild beasts. When I came back that night I was covered from head to foot with the blood and brains of that German. We had nothing personally against each other. He did not want to kill me any more than I wanted to kill him. That is war. I did my duty in it, but for God's sake do not ask me to talk about it! I want to forget it." That is war, and no more damning influence can be thrown around the characters of people in general or around the victims of military discipline and experience in particular than that supplied by war. How then could inconsistency be made more extreme than by saying that Christianity is concerned about the souls of men but is not concerned about international good-will and co-operation? After all, the approaches to the human problem from without in and from within out are not antithetical, but supplementary. This tunnel must be dug from both ends and until the Church thoroughly grasps that fact she will lead an incomplete and ineffectual life.

The purposes of Christianity involve social reform, not only, as we have said, because we must accomplish environmental change if we are to achieve widespread individual transformation, but also because we must reorganize social life and the ideas that underlie it if we are to maintain and get adequately expressed the individual's Christian spirit when once he has been transformed. Granted a man with an inwardly remotived life, sincerely desirous of living Christianly, see what a situation faces him in the present organization of our economic world! Selfishness consists in facing any human relationship with the main intent of getting from it for oneself all the pleasure and profit that one can. There are folk who use their families so. They live like parasites on the beautiful institution of family life, getting as much as possible for as little as possible. There are folk who use the nation so. To them their country is a gigantic grab-bag from which their greedy hands may snatch civic security and commercial gain. For such we have hard and bitter names. There is, however, one relationship — business — where we take for granted this very attitude which everywhere else we heartily condemn. Multitudes of folk go up to that central human relationship with the frank and unabashed confession that their primary motive is to make out of it all that they can for themselves. They never have organized their motives around the idea that the major meaning of business is public service.

The fact is, however, that all around us forms of business already have developed where we count it shame for a man to be chiefly motived by a desire for private gain. If you thought that the preacher were in love with his purse more than with his Gospel, you would not come again to hear him, and you would be right; if you thought that the teacher of your children cared for payday first and for teaching second, you would find another teacher for them tomorrow, and you ought to; if you thought that your physician cared more for his fees than he did for his patients, you would discharge him to-night and seek for a man more worthy of his high profession; if you had reason to suppose that the judges of the Supreme Court in Washington cared more for their salary than they did for justice, you could not easily measure your indignation and your shame. In the development of human life few things are nobler than the growth of the professional spirit, where in wide areas of enterprise, not private gain, but fine workmanship and public service have become the major motives. If one says that a sharp line of distinction is to be drawn between what we call professions and what we call business, he does not know history. Nursing, as a gainful calling, a hundred years ago was a mercenary affair into which undesirable people went for what they could get out of it. If nursing to-day is a great profession, where pride of workmanship and love of service increasingly are in control, it is because Florence Nightingale, and a noble company after her, have insisted that nursing essentially is service and that all nurses ought to organize their motives around that idea.

What is the essential difference between professions and business? Why should the building of a schoolhouse be a carnival of private profit for labourers and contractors alike, when the teaching in it is expected to be full of the love of fine workmanship and the joy of usefulness? Why, when a war is on, must the making of munitions here be a wild debauch of private profits, but the firing of them "over there" be a matter of self-forgetful sacrifice? Why, in selling a food which is essential to health, should the head of a sugar corporation say with impunity, "I think it is fair to get out of the consumers all you can, consistent with the business proposition," when the physician is expected to care for the undernourished with a devoted professional spirit utterly different from the sugar magnate's words? There is no real answer to that "why." The fact is that for multitudes of people business is still in the unredeemed state in which nursing and teaching and doctoring were at the beginning, and nothing can save us from the personal and social consequence of this unhappy situation except the clear vision of the basic meaning of business in terms of service, and the courageous reorganization of personal motive and economic institutions around that idea.

If, then, Christianity is sincerely interested in the quality of human spirits, in the motives and ideals which dominate personality, she must be interested in the economic and industrial problems of our day. To be sure, many ministers make fools of themselves when they pass judgment on questions which they do not understand. It is true that a church is much more peaceable and undisturbing when it tries experiments upon religious emotions with colored lights than when it makes reports upon the steel trust. Many are tempted, therefore, to give in to irritation over misdirected ministerial energy or to a desire for emotional comfort rather than an aroused conscience. One has only to listen where respectable folk most congregate to hear the cry: let the Church keep her hands off!

Let me talk for a moment directly to that group. If you mean, by your distaste for the Church's interest in a fairer economic life, that most ministers are unfitted by temperament and training to talk wisely on economic policies and programs, you are right. Do you suppose that we ministers do not know how we must appear to you when we try to discuss the details of business? While, however, you are free to say anything you wish about the ineptitude of ministers in economic affairs (and we, from our inside information, will probably agree with you), yet as we thus put ourselves in your places and try to see the situation through your eyes, do you also put yourselves in our places and try to see it through our eyes!

I speak, I am sure, in the name of thousands of Christian ministers in this country endeavouring to do their duty in this trying time. We did not go into the ministry of Jesus Christ either for money or for fun. If we had wanted either one primarily, we would have done something else than preach. We went in because we believed in Jesus Christ and were assured that only he and his truth could medicine the sorry ills of this sick world. And now, ministers of Christ, with such a motive, we see continually some of the dearest things we work for, some of the fairest results that we achieve, going to pieces on the rocks of the business world.

You wish us to preach against sin, but you forget that, as one of our leading sociologists has said, the master iniquities of our time are connected with money-making. You wish us to imbue your boys and girls with ideal standards of life, but all too often we see them, having left our schools and colleges, full of the knightly chivalry of youth, torn in the world of business between the ideal of Christlikeness and the selfish rivalry of commercial conflict. We watch them growing sordid, disillusioned, mercenary, spoiled at last and bereft of their youth's fine promise. You wish us to preach human brotherhood in Christ, and then we see that the one chief enemy of brotherhood between men and nations is economic strife, the root of class consciousness and war. You send some of us as your representatives to the ends of the earth to proclaim the Saviour, and then these missionaries send back word that the non-Christian world knows all too well how far from dominant in our business life our Christian ideals are and that the non-Christian world delays accepting our Christ until we have better proved that his principles will work. Everywhere that the Christian minister turns, he finds his dearest ideals and hopes entangled in the economic life. Do you ask us then under these conditions to keep our hands off? In God's name, you ask too much!

In the sixteenth century the great conflict in the world's life centered in the Church. The Reformation was on. All the vital questions of the day had there their spring. In the eighteenth century the great conflict of the world's life lay in politics. The American and French revolutions were afoot. Democracy had struck its tents and was on the march. All the vital questions of that day had their origin there. In the twentieth century the great conflict in the world's life is centered in economics. The most vital questions with which we deal are entangled with economic motives and institutions. As in the sixteenth and eighteenth centuries great changes were inevitable, so now the economic world cannot possibly remain static. The question is not whether changes will occur, but how they will occur, under whose aegis and superintendence, by whose guidance and direction, and how much better the world will be when they are here. Among all the interests that are vitally concerned with the nature of these changes none has more at stake than the Christian Church with her responsibility for the cure of souls.

V

Still another point of contact exists between the Christian purpose and social reform: the inevitable demand of religious ideals for social application. The ideal of human equality, for example, came into our civilization from two main sources — the Stoic philosophy and the Christian religion — and in both cases it was first of all a spiritual insight, not a social program. The Stoics and the early Christians both believed it as a sentiment, but they had no idea of changing the world to conform with it. Paul repeatedly insisted upon the equality of all men before God. In his early ministry he wrote it to the Galatians: "There can be neither Jew nor Greek, there can be neither bond nor free, there can be no male and female; for ye all are one man in Christ Jesus." Later he wrote it to the Corinthians: "For in one Spirit were we all baptized into one body, whether Jews or Greeks, whether bond or free; and were all made to drink of one Spirit." In his last imprisonment he wrote it to the Colossians: "There cannot be Greek and Jew, circumcision and uncircumcision, barbarian, Scythian, bondman, freeman; but Christ is all, and in all." Yet it never would have occurred to Paul to disturb the social custom of slavery or to question the divine institution of imperial government.

Nevertheless, while this idea of human equality did not at first involve a social program, it meant something real. If we are to understand what the New Testament means by the equality of men before God, we must look at men from the New Testament point of view. Those of us who have been up in an aeroplane know that the higher we fly the less difference we see in the elevation of things upon the earth. This man's house is plainly higher than that man's when we are on the ground but, two thousand feet up, small difference can we observe. Now, the New Testament flies high. It frankly looks from a great altitude at the distinctions that seem so important on the earth. We say that racial differences are very important — a great gulf between Jew and Gentile. We insist that cultural traditions make an immense distinction — that to be a Scythian or to be barbarian is widely separated from being Greek. We are sure that the economic distinction between bondman and freeman is enormous. But all the while these superiorities and inferiorities, which we magnify, seem from Paul's vantage point not nearly so important or so real as we think they are. He is sure about this central truth, that God asks no questions about caste or colour or race or wealth or social station. All men stand alike in his presence and in the Christian fellowship must be regarded from his point of view.

It was utterly impossible, however, to keep this spiritual insight from getting ultimately into a social program. It appealed to motives too deep and powerful to make possible its segregation as a religious sentiment. For however impractical an ideal this thought of human equality may seem in general, and however hard it may be to grant to others in particular, it is never hard for us to claim for ourselves. If ever we are condescended to, does any assertion rise more quickly in our thought than the old cry of our boyhood, "I am as good as you are"? The lad in school in ragged clothes, who sees himself outclassed by richer boys, feels it hotly rising in his boyish heart: "I am as good as you are." The poor man who, with an anxiety he cannot subdue and yet dares not disclose, is desperately trying to make both ends meet, feels it as he sees more fortunate men in luxury: "I am as good as you are." The negro who has tried himself out with his white brethren, who wears, it may be, an honour key from a great university, who is a scholar and a gentleman, and yet who is continually denied the most common courtesies of human intercourse—he says in his heart, although the words may not pass his lips, "I am as good as you are." Now, the New Testament took that old cry of the human heart for equality and turned it upside down. It became no longer for the Christian a bitter demand for one's rights, but a glad acknowledgment of one's duty. It did not clamour, "I am as good as you are"; it said, "You are as good as I am." The early Christians at their best went out into the world with that cry upon their lips. The Jewish Christians said it to the Gentiles and the Gentiles to the Jews; the Scythians and barbarians said it to the Greeks and the Greeks said it in return; the bond said it to the free and the free said it to the bond. The New Testament Church in this regard was one of the most extraordinary upheavals in history, and to-day the best hopes of the world depend upon that spirit which still says to all men over all the differences of race and colour and station, "You are as good as I am."

To be sure, before this equalitarian ideal could be embodied in a social program it had to await the coming of the modern age with its open doors, its freer movements of thought and life, its belief in progress, its machinery of change. But even in the stagnation of the intervening centuries the old Stoic-Christian ideal never was utterly forgotten. Lactantius, a Christian writer of the fourth century, said that God, who creates and inspires men, "willed that all should be equal." Gregory the Great, at the end of the sixth century, said that "By nature we are all equal." For ages this spiritual insight remained dissociated from any social program, but now the inevitable connection has been made. Old caste systems and chattel slavery have gone down before this ideal. Aristotle argued that slavery ethically was right because men were essentially and unchangeably masters or slaves by nature. Somehow that would not sound plausible to us, even though the greatest mind of all antiquity did say it. Whatever may be the differences between men and races, they are not sufficient to justify the ownership of one man by another. The ideal of equality has wrecked old aristocracies that seemed to have firm hold on permanence. If one would feel again the thrill which men felt when first the old distinctions lost their power, one should read once more the songs of Robert Burns. They often seem commonplaces to us now, but they were not commonplaces then:

"For a' that and a' that,

Their dignities, and a' that;

The pith o' sense and pride o' worth

Are higher rank than a' that!"

This ideal has made equality before the law one of the maxims of our civilized governments, failure in which wakens our apprehension and our fear; it has made equal suffrage a fact, although practical people only yesterday laughed at it as a dream; it has made equality in opportunity for an education the underlying postulate of our public school systems, although in New York State seventy-five years ago the debate was still acute as to whether such a dream ever could come true; it is to-day lifting races, long accounted inferior, to an eminence where increasingly their equality is acknowledged. One with difficulty restrains his scorn for the intellectual impotence of so-called wise men who think all idealists mere dreamers. Who is the dreamer—the despiser or the upholder of an ideal whose upheavals already have burst through old caste systems, upset old slave systems, wrecked old aristocracies, pushed obscure and forgotten masses of mankind up to rough equality in court and election booth and school, and now are rocking the foundations of old racial and international and economic ideas? The practical applications of this ideal, as, for example, to the coloured problem in America, are so full of difficulty that no one need be ashamed to confess that he does not see in detail how the principle can be made to work. Nevertheless, so deep in the essential nature of things is the fact of mankind's fundamental unity, that only God can foresee to what end the application of it yet may come. At any rate, it is clear that the Christian ideal of human equality before God can no longer be kept out of a social program.

VI

There is, then, no standing-ground left for a narrowly individualistic Christianity. To talk of redeeming personality while one is careless of the social environments which ruin personality; to talk of building Christlike character while one is complacent about an economic system that is definitely organized about the idea of selfish profit; to praise Christian ideals while one is blind to the inevitable urgency with which they insist on getting themselves expressed in social programs—all this is vanity. It is deplorable, therefore, that the Christian forces are tempted to draw apart, some running up the banner of personal regeneration and some rallying around the flag of social reformation. The division is utterly needless. Doubtless our own individual ways of coming into the Christian life influence us deeply here. Some of us came into the Christian experience from a sense of individual need alone. We needed for ourselves sins forgiven, peace restored, hope bestowed. God meant to us first of all satisfaction for our deepest personal wants.

"Rock of Ages, cleft for me,

Let me hide myself in Thee"—

such was our cry and such was our salvation. If now we are socially minded, if we are concerned for economic and international righteousness, that is an enlargement of our Christian outlook which has grown out of and still is rooted back in our individual need and experience of God.

Some of us, however, did not come into fellowship with God by that route at all. We came in from the opposite direction. The character in the Old Testament who seems to me the worthiest exhibition of personal religion before Jesus is the prophet Jeremiah, but Jeremiah started his religious experience, not with a sense of individual need, but with a burning, patriotic, social passion. He was concerned for Judah. Her iniquities, long accumulating, were bringing upon her an irretrievable disaster. He laid his soul upon her soul and sought to breathe into her the breath of life. Then, when he saw the country he adored, the civilization he cherished, crashing into ruin, he was thrown back personally on God. He started with social passion; he ended with social passion plus personal religion. Some of God's greatest servants have come to know him so.

Henry Ward Beecher once said that a text is a small gate into a large field where one can wander about as he pleases, and that the trouble with most ministers is that they spend all their time swinging on the gate. That same figure applies to the entrance which many of us made into the Christian experience. Some of us came in by the gate of personal religion, and we have been swinging on it ever since; and some of us came in by the gate of social passion for the regeneration of the world, and we have been swinging on that gate ever since. We both are wrong. These are two gates into the same city, and it is the city of our God. It would be one of the greatest blessings to the Christian church both at home and on the foreign field if we could come together on this question where separation is so needless and so foolish. If some of us started with emphasis upon personal religion, we have no business to stop until we understand the meaning of social Christianity. If some of us started with emphasis upon the social campaign, we have no business to rest until we learn the deep secrets of personal religion. The redemption of personality is the great aim of the Christian Gospel, and, therefore, to inspire the inner lives of men and to lift outward burdens which impede their spiritual growth are both alike Christian service to bring in the Kingdom.

LECTURE IV
PROGRESSIVE CHRISTIANITY
I

Hitherto in the development of our thought, we have been considering the Christian Gospel as an entity set in the midst of a progressive world, and we have been studying the new Christian attitudes which this influential environment has been eliciting. The Gospel has been in our thought like an individual who, finding himself in novel circumstances, reacts toward them in ways appropriate alike to them and to his own character. The influence of the idea of progress upon Christianity, however, is more penetrating than such a figure can adequately portray. For no one can long ponder the significance of our generation's progressive ways of thinking without running straight upon this question: is not Christianity itself progressive? In the midst of a changing world does not it also change, so that, reacting upon the new ideas of progress, it not only assimilates and uses them, but is itself an illustration of them? Where everything else in man's life in its origin and growth is conceived, not in terms of static and final creation or revelation, but in terms of development, can religion be left out? Instead of being a pond around which once for all a man can walk and take its measure, a final and completed whole, is not Christianity a river which, maintaining still reliance upon the historic springs from which it flows, gathers in new tributaries on its course and is itself a changing, growing and progressive movement? The question is inevitable in any study of the relationship between the Gospel and progress, and its implications are so far-reaching that it deserves our careful thought.

Certainly it is clear that already modern ideas of progress have had so penetrating an influence upon Christianity as to affect, not its external reactions and methods only, nor yet its intellectual formulations alone, but deeper still its very mood and inward temper. Whether or not Christianity ought to be a changing movement in a changing world, it certainly has been that and is so still, and the change can be seen going on now in the very atmosphere in which it lives and moves and has its being. For example, consider the attitude of resignation to the will of God, which was characteristic of medieval Christianity. As we saw in our first lecture, the medieval age did not think of human life upon this earth in terms of progress. The hopes of men did not revolve about any Utopia to be expected here. History was not even a glacier, moving slowly toward the sunny meadows. It did not move at all; it was not intended to move; it was standing still. To be sure, the thirteenth century was one of the greatest in the annals of the race. In it the foremost European universities were founded, the sublimest Gothic cathedrals were built, some of the world's finest works of handicraft were made; in it Cimabue and Giotto painted, Dante wrote, St. Thomas Aquinas philosophized, and St. Francis of Assisi lived. The motives, however, which originated and sustained this magnificent outburst of creative energy were otherworldly — they were not concerned with anticipations of a happier lot for humankind upon this earth. The medieval age did not believe that man's estate upon the earth ever would be fundamentally improved, and in consequence took the only reasonable attitude, resignation. When famines came, God sent them; they were punishment for sin; his will be done! When wars came, they were the flails of God to thresh his people; his will be done! Men were resigned to slavery on the ground that God had made men to be masters and slaves. They were resigned to feudalism and absolute monarchy on the ground that God had made men to be rulers and ruled. Whatever was had been ordained by the Divine or had been allowed by him in punishment for man's iniquity. To rebel was sin; to doubt was heresy; to submit was piety. The Hebrew prophets had not been resigned, nor Jesus Christ, nor Paul. The whole New Testament blazes with the hope of the kingdom of righteousness coming upon earth. But the medieval age was resigned. Its real expectations were post-mortem hopes. So far as this earth was concerned, men must submit.

To be sure, in those inner experiences where we must endure what we cannot help, resignation will always characterize a deeply religious life. All life is not under our control, to be freely mastered by our thought and toil. There are areas where scientific knowledge gives us power to do amazing things, but all around them are other areas which our hands cannot regulate. Orion and the Pleiades were not made for our fingers to swing, and our engineering does not change sunrise or sunset nor make the planets one whit less or more. So, in the experiences of our inward life, around the realm which we can control is that other realm where move the mysterious providences of God, beyond our power to understand and as uncontrollable by us as the tides are by the fish that live in them. Captain Scott found the South Pole, only to discover that another man had been there first. When, on his return from the disappointing quest, the pitiless cold, the endless blizzards, the failing food, had worn down the strength of the little company and in their tent amid the boundless desolation they waited for the end while the life flames burned low, Captain Scott wrote: "I do not regret this journey. . . . We took risks, we knew we took them; things have come out against us, and therefore we have no cause for complaint, but bow to the will of Providence, determined still to do our best to the last." That is resignation at its noblest.

When, however, a modern Christian tries to do what the medieval Christians did—make this attitude of resignation cover the whole field of life, make it the dominant element in their religion, the proof of their trust and the test of their piety—he finds himself separated from the most characteristic and stirring elements in his generation. We are not resigned anywhere else. Everywhere else we count it our pride and glory to be unresigned. We are not resigned even to a thorny cactus, whose spiky exterior seems a convincing argument against its use for food. When we see a barren plain we do not say as our fathers did: God made plains so in his inscrutable wisdom; his will be done! We call for irrigation and, when the fructifying waters flow, we say, Thy will be done! in the way we think God wishes to have it said. We do not passively submit to God's will; we actively assert it. The scientific control of life at this point has deeply changed our religious mood. We are not resigned to pestilences and already have plans drawn up to make the yellow fever germ "as extinct as the woolly rhinoceros." We are not even resigned to the absence of wireless telephony when once we have imagined its presence, or to the inconvenience of slow methods of travel when once we have invented swift ones. Not to illiteracy nor to child labour nor to the white plague nor to commercialized vice nor to recurrent unemployment are we, at our best, resigned.

This change of mood did not come easily. So strongly did the medieval spirit of resignation, submissive in a static world, keep its grip upon the Church that the Church often defiantly withstood the growth of this unresigned attitude of which we have been speaking and in which we glory. Lightning rods were vehemently denounced by many ministers as an unwarranted interference with God's use of lightning. When God hit a house he meant to hit it; his will be done! This attitude, thus absurdly applied, had in more important realms a lamentable consequence. The campaign of Christian missions to foreign lands was bitterly fought in wide areas of the Christian Church because if God intended to damn the heathen he should be allowed to do so without interference from us; his will be done! As for slavery, the last defense which it had in this country was on religious grounds: that God had ordained it and that it was blasphemous to oppose his ordination. In a word, this spirit of passive resignation has been so deeply ingrained in religious thinking that it has become oftentimes a serious reproach to Christian people.

Now, however, the mood of modern Christianity is decisively in contrast with that medieval spirit. Moreover, we think that we are close to the Master in this attitude, for whatever difference in outward form of expectation there may be between his day and ours, when he said: "Thy kingdom come. Thy will be done, as in heaven, so on earth," that was not passive submission to God's will but an aggressive prayer for the victory of God and righteousness; it was not lying down under the will of God as something to be endured, but active loyalty to the will of God as something to be achieved. To be resigned to evil conditions on this earth is in our eyes close to essential sin. If any one who calls himself a conservative Christian doubts his share in this anti-medieval spirit, let him test himself and see. In 1836 the Rev. Leonard Wood, D. D., wrote down this interesting statement: "I remember when I could reckon up among my acquaintances forty ministers, and none of them at a great distance, who were either drunkards or far addicted to drinking. I could mention an ordination which took place about twenty years ago at which I myself was ashamed and grieved to see two aged ministers literally drunk, and a third indecently excited." Our forefathers were resigned to that, but we are not. The most conservative of us so hates the colossal abomination of the liquor traffic, that we do not propose to cease our fight until victory has been won. We are belligerently unresigned. Or when militarism proves itself an intolerable curse, we do not count it a divine punishment and prepare ourselves to make the best of its continuance. We propose to end it. Militarism, which in days of peace cries, Build me vast armaments, spend enough upon a single dreadnaught to remake the educational system of a whole state; militarism, which in the days of war cries, Give me your best youth to slay, leave the crippled and defective to propagate the race, give me your best to slay; militarism, which lays its avaricious hand on every new invention to make gregarious death more swift and terrible, and when war is over makes the starved bodies of innumerable children walk in its train for pageantry, — we are not resigned to that. We count it our Christian duty to be tirelessly unresigned.

Here is a new mood in Christianity, born out of the scientific control of life and the modern ideas of progress, and, however consonant it may be with the spirit of the New Testament, it exhibits in the nature of its regulative conceptions and in its earthly hopes a transformation within Christianity which penetrates deep. Progressive change is not simply an environment to which Christianity conforms; it is a fact which Christianity exhibits.

II

This idea that Christianity is itself a progressive movement instead of a static finality involves some serious alterations in the historic conceptions of the faith, as soon as it is applied to theology. Very early in Christian history the presence of conflicting heresies led the church to define its faith in creeds and then to regard these as final formulations of Christian doctrine, incapable of amendment or addition. Tertullian, about 204 A. D., spoke of the creedal standard of his day as "a rule of faith changeless and incapable of reformation." From that day until our own, when a Roman Catholic Council has decreed that "the definitions of the Roman Pontiff are unchangeable," an unalterable character has been ascribed to the dogmas of the Church of Rome. Indeed, Pius IX, in his Syllabus of Errors, specifically condemned the modern idea that "Divine revelation is imperfect, and, therefore, subject to continual and indefinite progress, which corresponds with the progress of human reason." Nor did Protestantism, with all the reformation which it wrought, attack this central Catholic conception of a changeless content and formulation of faith. Not what the Pope said, but what the Bible said, was by Protestants unalterably to be received. Change there might be in the sense that unrealized potentialities involved in the original deposit might be brought to light—a kind of development which not only Protestants but Catholics like Cardinal Newman have willingly allowed—but whatever had once been stated as the content of faith by the received authorities was by both Catholics and Protestants regarded as unalterably so. In the one case, if the Pope had once defined a dogma, it was changeless; in the other, if the Bible had once formulated a pre-scientific cosmology, or used demoniacal possession as an explanation of disease, or personified evil in a devil, all such mental categories were changelessly to be received. In its popular forms this conception of Christianity assumes extreme rigidity— Christianity is a static system finally formulated, a deposit to be accepted in toto if at all, not to be added to, not to be subtracted from, not to be changed, its i's all dotted and its t's all crossed.

The most crucial problem which we face in our religious thinking is created by the fact that Christianity thus statically conceived now goes out into a generation where no other aspect of life is conceived in static terms at all. The earth itself on which we live, not by fiat suddenly enacted, but by long and gradual processes, became habitable, and man upon it through uncounted ages grew out of an unknown past into his present estate. Everything within man's life has grown, is growing, and apparently will grow. Music developed from crude forms of rhythmic noise until now, by way of Bach, Beethoven and Wagner, our modern music, still developing, has grown to forms of harmony at first undreamed. Painting developed from the rough outlines of the cavemen until now possibilities of expression in line and colour have been achieved whose full expansion we cannot guess. Architecture evolved from the crude huts of primitive man until now our cathedrals and our new business buildings alike mark an incalculable advance and prophesy an unimaginable future. One may refuse to call all development real progress, may insist upon degeneration as well as betterment through change, but, even so, the basic fact remains that all the elements which go to make man's life come into being, are what they are, and pass out of what they are into something different, through processes of continual growth. Our business methods change until the commercial wisdom of a few years ago may be the folly of to-day; our moral ideals change until actions once respectable become reprobate, and the heroes of one generation would be the convicts of another; our science changes until ideas that men once were burned at the stake for entertaining are now the commonplace axioms of every school boy's thought; our economics change until schools of thought shaped to old industrial conditions are as outmoded as a one-horse shay beside an automobile; our philosophy changes like our science when Kant, for example, starts a revolution in man's thinking, worthy, as he claimed, to be called Copernican; our cultural habits change until marooned communities in the Kentucky mountains, "our contemporary ancestors," having let the stream of human life flow around and past them, seem as strange to us as a belated what-not in a modern parlour. The perception of this fact of progressive change is one of the regnant influences in our modern life and, strangely enough, so far from disliking it, we glory in it; in our expectancy we count on change; with our control of life we seek to direct it.

Indeed no more remarkable difference distinguishes the modern world from all that went before than its attitude toward change itself. The medieval world idealized changelessness. Its very astronomy was the apotheosis of the unalterable. The earth, a globe full of mutation and decay; around it eight transparent spheres carrying the heavenly bodies, each outer sphere moving more slowly than its inner neighbour, while the ninth, moving most slowly of all, moved all the rest; last of all, the empyrean, blessed with changeless, motionless perfection, the abode of God—such was the Ptolemaic astronomy as Dante knew it. This idealization of changelessness was the common property of all that by gone world. The Holy Roman Empire was the endeavour to perpetuate a changeless idea of political theory and organization; the Holy Catholic Church was the endeavour to perpetuate a changeless formulation of religious dogma and hierarchy; the Summa of St. Thomas Aquinas was the endeavour to settle forever changeless paths for the human mind to walk in. To that ancient world as a whole the perfect was the finished, and therefore it was immutable.

How different our modern attitude toward change has come to be! We believe in change, rely on it, hope for it, rejoice in it, are determined to achieve it and control it. Nowhere is this more evident than in our thought of the meaning of knowledge. In the medieval age knowledge was spun as a spider spins his web. Thinking simply made evident what already was involved in an accepted proposition. A premise was drawn out into its filaments and then woven into a fabric of new form but of the same old material. Knowledge did not start from actual things; it did not intend to change actual things; and the shelves of the libraries groan with the burden of that endless and largely futile cogitation. Then the new knowledge began from the observation of things as they really are and from the use of that observation for the purposes of human life. Once a lad, seventeen years old, went into the cathedral at Pisa to worship. Soon he forgot the service and watched a chandelier, swinging from the lofty roof. He wondered whether, no matter how changeable the length of its arc, its oscillations always consumed the same time and, because he had no other means, he timed its motion by the beating of his pulse. That was one time when a boy went to church and did well to forget the service. He soon began to wonder whether he could not make a pendulum which, swinging like the chandeliers, would do useful business for men. He soon began to discover, in what he had seen that day, new light on the laws of planetary motion. That was one of the turning points in human history—the boy was Galileo. The consequences of this new method are all around us now. The test of knowledge in modern life is capacity to cause change. If a man really knows electricity he can cause change; he can illumine cities and drive cars. If a man really knows engineering, he can cause change; he can tunnel rivers and bridge gulfs. It is for that purpose we wish knowledge. Instead of being dreaded, controlled change has become the chief desire of modern life.

When, therefore, in this generation with its perception of growth as the universal law and with its dependence upon controlled change as the hope of man, Christianity endeavours to glorify changelessness and to maintain itself in unalterable formulations, it has outlawed itself from its own age. An Indian punkah-puller, urged by his mistress to better his condition, replied: "Mem Sahib, my father pulled a punkah, my grandfather pulled a punkah, all my ancestors for four million ages pulled punkahs, and, before that, the god who founded our caste pulled a punkah over Vishnu." How utterly lost such a man would be in the dynamic movements of our modern Western life!—yet not more lost than is a Christianity which tries to remain static in a progressive world.

III

Among the influences which have forced well-instructed minds first to accept and then to glory in the progressive nature of Christianity, the first place must be given to the history of religion itself. The study of religion's ancient records in ritual, monument and book, and of primitive faiths still existing among us in all stages of development, has made clear the general course which man's religious life has traveled from very childish beginnings until now. From early animism in its manifold expressions, through polytheism, kathenotheism, henotheism, to monotheism, and so out into loftier possibilities of conceiving the divine nature and purpose—the main road which man has traveled in his religious development now is traceable. Nor is there any place where it is more easily traceable than in our own Hebrew-Christian tradition. One of the fine results of the historical study of the Scriptures is the possibility which now exists of arranging the manuscripts of the Bible in approximately chronological order and then tracing through them the unfolding growth of the faiths and hopes which come to their flower in the Gospel of Christ. Consider, for example, the exhilarating story of the developing conception of Jehovah's character from the time he was worshiped as a mountain-god in the desert until he became known as the "God and Father of our Lord Jesus Christ."

We are explicitly told that the history of Jehovah's relationship with Israel began at Sinai and that before that time the Hebrew fathers had never even heard his name. There on a mountain-top in the Sinaitic wilderness dwelt this new-found god, so anthropomorphically conceived that he could hide Moses in a rock's cleft from which the prophet could not see Jehovah's face but could see his back. He was a god of battle and the name of an old book about him still remains to us, "The book of the Wars of Jehovah."

"Jehovah is a man of war:

Jehovah is his name"—

so his people at first rejoiced in him and gloried in his power when he thundered and lightened on Sinai. Few stories in man's spiritual history are so interesting as the record of the way in which this mountain-god, for the first time, so far as we know, in Semitic history, left his settled shrine, traveled with his people in the holy Ark, became acclimated in Canaan, and, gradually absorbing the functions of the old baals of the land, extended his sovereignty over the whole of Palestine.

To be sure, even then he still was thought of, as all ancient gods were thought of, as geographically limited to the country whose god he was. Milcolm and Chemosh were real gods too, ruling in Philistia and Moab as Jehovah did in Canaan. This is the meaning of Jephthah's protest to a hostile chieftain: "Wilt not thou possess that which Chemosh thy god giveth thee to possess?" This is the meaning of David's protest when he is driven out to the Philistine cities: "They have driven me out this day that I should not cleave unto the inheritance of Jehovah, saying, Go, serve other gods." This is the meaning of Naaman's desire to have two mules' burden of Jehovah's land on which to worship Jehovah in Damascus. Jehovah could be worshiped only on Jehovah's land. But ever as the day of fuller understanding dawned, the sovereignty of Jehovah widened and his power usurped the place and function of all other gods. Amos saw him using the nations as his pawns; Isaiah heard him whistling to the nations as a shepherd to his dogs; Jeremiah heard him cry, "Can any hide himself in secret places so that I shall not see him? . . . Do not I fill heaven and earth?" ; until at last we sweep out, through the exile and all the heightening of faith and clarifying of thought that came with it, into the Great Isaiah's 40th chapter on the universal and absolute sovereignty of God, into the Priestly narrative of creation, where God makes all things with a word, into psalms which cry,

"For all the gods of the people are idols;

But Jehovah made the heavens."

Moreover, as Jehovah's sovereignty thus is enlarged until he is the God of all creation, his character too is deepened and exalted in the understanding of his people. That noblest succession of moral teachers in ancient history, the Hebrew prophets, developed a conception of the nature of God in terms of righteousness, so broad in its outreach, so high in its quality, that as one mounts through Amos' fifth chapter and Isaiah's first chapter and Jeremiah's seventh chapter, he finds himself, like Moses on Nebo's top, looking over into the Promised Land of the New Testament. There this development flowers out under the influence of Jesus. God's righteousness is interpreted, not in terms of justice only, but of compassionate, sacrificial love; his Fatherhood embraces not only all mankind but each individual, lifting him out of obscurity in the mass into infinite worthfulness and hope. And more than this development of idea, the New Testament gives us a new picture of God in the personality of Jesus, and we see the light of the knowledge of God's glory in his face.

Moreover, this development, so plainly recorded in Scripture, was not unconsciously achieved by the drift of circumstance; it represents the ardent desire of forward-looking men, inspired by the Spirit. The Master, himself, was consciously pleading for a progressive movement in the religious life and thinking of his day. A static religion was the last thing he ever dreamed of or wanted. No one was more reverent than he toward his people's past; his thought and his speech were saturated with the beauty of his race's heritage; yet consider his words as again and again they fell from his lips: "It was said to them of old time . . . but I say unto you." His life was rooted in the past but it was not imprisoned there; it grew up out of the past, not destroying but fulfilling it. He had in him the spirit of the prophets, who once had spoken to his people in words of fire; but old forms that he thought had been outgrown he brushed aside. He would not have his Gospel a patch on an old garment, he said, nor would he put it like new wine into old wineskins. He appealed from the oral traditions of the elders to the written law; within the written law he distinguished between ceremonial and ethical elements, making the former of small or no account, the latter all-important; and then within the written ethical law he waived provisions that seemed to him outmoded by time. Even when he bade farewell to his disciples, he did not talk to them as if what he himself had said were a finished system: "I have yet many things to say unto you, but ye cannot bear them now. Howbeit when he, the Spirit of truth, is come, he shall guide you into all the truth."

In Paul's hands the work which Jesus began went on. He dared an adventurous move that makes much of our modern progressiveness look like child's play: he lifted the Christian churches out of the narrow, religious exclusiveness of the Hebrew synagogue. He dared to wage battle for the new idea that Christianity was not a Jewish sect but a universal religion. He withstood to his face Peter, still trammeled in the narrowness of his Jewish thinking, and he founded churches across the Roman Empire where was neither Jew nor Greek, barbarian, Scythian, male nor female, bond nor free, but all were one man in Christ Jesus.

Even more thrilling were those later days when in Ephesus the writer of the Fourth Gospel faced a Hellenistic audience, to whom the forms of thought in which Jesus hitherto had been interpreted were utterly unreal. The first creed about Jesus proclaimed that he was the Messiah, but Messiah was a Jewish term and to the folk of Ephesus it had no vital meaning. John could not go on calling the Master that and that alone, when he had hungry souls before him who needed the Master but to whom Jewish terms had no significance. One thing those folk of Ephesus did understand, the idea of the Logos. They had heard of that from the many faiths whose pure or syncretized forms made the religious background of their time. They knew about the Logos from Zoroastrianism, where beside Ahura Mazdah stood Vohu Manah, the Mind of God; from Stoicism, at the basis of whose philosophy lay the idea of the Logos; from Alexandrian

Hellenism, by means of which a Jew like Philo had endeavoured to marry Greek philosophy and Hebrew orthodoxy. And the writer of the Fourth Gospel used that new form of thought in which to present to his people the personality of our Lord. "In the beginning was the Logos, and the Logos was with God, and the Logos was God"—so begins the Fourth Gospel's prologue, in words that every intelligent person in Ephesus could understand and was familiar with, and that initial sermon in the book, for it is a sermon, not philosophy, moves on in forms of thought which the people knew about and habitually used, until the hidden purpose comes to light: "The Logos became flesh and dwelt among us (and we beheld his glory, glory as of the only begotten from the Father), full of grace and truth." John was presenting his Lord to the people of his time in terms that the people could understand.

Even within the New Testament, therefore, there is no static creed. For, like a flowing river, the Church's thought of her Lord shaped itself to the intellectual banks of the generation through which it moved, even while, by its construction and erosion, it transfigured them. Nor did this movement cease with New Testament days. From the Johannine idea of the Logos to the Nicene Creed, where our Lord is set in the framework of Greek metaphysics, the development is just as clear as from the category of Jewish Messiah to the categories of the Fourth Gospel. And if, in our generation, a conservative scholar like the late Dr. Sanday pleaded for the necessity of a new Christology, it was not because he was primarily zealous for a novel philosophy, but because like John of old in Ephesus he was zealous to present Christ to his own generation in terms that his own generation could comprehend.

IV

Undoubtedly such an outlook upon the fluid nature of the Christian movement will demand readjustment in the religious thinking of many people. They miss the old ideas about revelation. This new progressiveness seems to them to be merely the story of man's discovery, finding God, here a little and there a little, as he has found the truths of astronomy. But God's revelation of himself is just as real when it is conceived in progressive as when it is conceived in static terms. Men once thought of God's creation of the world in terms of fiat — it was done on the instant; and when evolution was propounded men cried that the progressive method shut God out. We see now how false that fear was. The creative activity of God never was so nobly conceived as it has been since we have known the story of his slow unfolding of the universe. We have a grander picture in our minds than even the psalmist had, when we say after him, "The heavens declare the glory of God." So men who have been accustomed to think of revelation in static terms, now that the long leisureliness of man's developing spiritual insight is apparent, fear that this does away with revelation. But in God's unfolding education of his people recorded in the Scriptures revelation is at its noblest. No man ever found God except when God was seeking to be found. Discovery is the under side of the process; the upper side is revelation.

Indeed, this conception of progressive revelation does not shut out finality. In scientific thought, which continually moves and grows, expands and changes, truths are discovered once for all. The work of Copernicus is in a real sense final. This earth does move; it is not stationary; and the universe is not geocentric. That discovery is final. Many developments start from that, but the truth itself is settled once for all. So, in the spiritual history of man, final revelations come. They will not have to be made over again and they will not have to be given up. Progress does not shut out finality; it only makes each new finality a point of departure for a new adventure, not a terminus ad quem for a conclusive stop. That God was in Christ reconciling the world unto himself is for the Christian a finality, but, from the day the first disciples saw its truth until now, the intellectual formulations in which it has been set and the mental categories by which it has been interpreted have changed with the changes of each age's thought.

While at first, then, a progressive Christianity may seem to plunge us into unsettlement, the more one studies it the less he would wish it otherwise. Who would accept a snapshot taken at any point on the road of Christian development as the final and perfect form of Christianity? Robert Louis Stevenson has drawn for us a picture of a man trying with cords and pegs to stake out the shadow of an oak tree, expecting that when he had marked its boundaries the shadow would stay within the limits of the pegs. Yet all the while the mighty globe was turning around in space. He could not keep a tree's shadow static on a moving earth. Nevertheless, multitudes of people in their endeavour to build up an infallibly settled creed have tried just such a hopeless task. They forget that while a revelation from God might conceivably be final and complete, religion deals with a revelation of God. God, the infinite and eternal, from everlasting to everlasting, the source and crown and destiny of all the universe—shall a man whose days are as grass rise up to say that he has made a statement about him which will not need to be revised? Rather, our prayer should be that the thought of God, the meaning of God, the glory of God, the plans and purpose of God may expand in our comprehension until we, who now see in a mirror, darkly, may see face to face. "Le Dieu défini est le Dieu fini."

This mistaken endeavour, in the interest of stability, to make a vital movement static is not confined to religion. Those of us who love Wagner remember the lesson of Die Meistersinger. Down in Nuremberg they had standardized and conventionalized music. They had set it down in rules and men like Beckmesser could not imagine that there was any music permissible outside the regulations. Then came Walter von Stolzing. Music to him was not a conventionality but a passion—not a rule, but a life—and, when he sang, his melodies reached heights of beauty that Beckmesser's rules did not provide for. It was Walter von Stolzing who sang the Prize Song, and as the hearts of the people were stirred in answer to its spontaneous melody, until all the population of Nuremberg were singing its accumulating harmonies, poor Beckmesser on his blackboard jotted down the rules which were being broken. Beckmesser represents a static conception of life which endeavours to freeze progress at a given point and call it infallible. But Beckmesser is wrong. You cannot take things like music and religion and set them down in final rules and regulations. They are life, and you have to let them grow and flower and expand and reveal evermore the latent splendour at their heart.

V

Obviously, the point where this progressive conception of Christianity comes into conflict with many widely accepted ideas is the abandonment which it involves of an external and inerrant authority in matters of religion. The marvel is that that idea of authority, which is one of the historic curses of religion, should be regarded by so many as one of the vital necessities of the faith. The fact is that religion by its very nature is one of the realms to which external authority is least applicable. In science people commonly suppose that they do not take truth on any one's authority; they prove it. In business they do not accept methods on authority; they work them out. In statesmanship they no longer believe in the divine right of kings nor do they accept infallible dicta handed down from above. But they think that religion is delivered to them by authority and that they believe what they do believe because a divine Church or a divine Book or a divine Man told them.

In this common mode of thinking, popular ideas have the truth turned upside down. The fact is that science, not religion, is the realm where most of all we use external authority. They tell us that there are millions of solar systems scattered through the fields of space. Is that true? How do we know? We never counted them. We know only what the authorities say. They tell us that the next great problem in science is breaking up the atom to discover the incalculable resources of power there waiting to be harnessed by our skill. Is that true? Most of us do not understand what an atom is, and what it means to break one up passes the farthest reach of our imaginations; all we know is what the authorities say. They tell us that electricity is a mode of motion in ether. Is that true? Most of us have no first hand knowledge about electricity. The motorman calls it "juice" and that means as much to us as to call it a mode of motion in ether; we must rely on the authorities. They tell us that sometime we are going to talk through wireless telephones across thousands of miles, so that no man need ever be out of vocal communication with his family and friends. Is that true? It seems to us an incredible miracle, but we suppose that it is so, as the authorities say. In a word, the idea that we do not use authority in science is absurd. Science is precisely the place where nine hundred and ninety-nine men out of a thousand use authority the most. The chemistry, biology, geology, astronomy which the authorities teach is the only science which most of us possess.

There is another realm, however, where we never think of taking such an attitude. They tell us that friendship is beautiful. Is that true? Would we ever think of saying that we do not know, ourselves, but that we rely on the authorities? Far better to say that our experience with friendship has been unhappy and that we personally question its utility! That, at least, would have an accent of personal, original experience in it. For here we are facing a realm where we never can enter at all until we enter, each man for himself.

Two realms exist, therefore, in each of which first-hand experience is desirable, but in only one of which it is absolutely indispensable. We can live on what the authorities in physics say, but there are no proxies for the soul. Love, friendship, delight in music and in nature, parental affection—these things are like eating and breathing; no one can do them for us; we must enter the experience for ourselves. Religion, too, belongs in this last realm. The one vital thing in religion is first-hand, personal experience. Religion is the most intimate, inward, incommunicable fellowship of the human soul. In the words of Plotinus, religion is "the flight of the alone to the Alone." You never know God at all until you know him for yourself. The only God you ever will know is the God you do know for yourself.

This does not mean, of course, that there are no authorities in religion. There are authorities in everything, but the function of an authority in religion, as in every other vital realm, is not to take the place of our eyes, seeing in our stead and inerrantly declaring to us what it sees; the function of an authority is to bring to us the insight of the world's accumulated wisdom and the revelations of God's seers, and so to open our eyes that we may see, each man for himself. So an authority in literature does not say to his students: The Merchant of Venice is a great drama; you may accept my judgment on that—I know. Upon the contrary, he opens their eyes; he makes them see; he makes their hearts sensitive so that the genius which made Shylock and Portia live captivates and subdues them, until like the Samaritans they say, "Now we believe, not because of thy speaking: for we have heard for ourselves, and know." That is the only use of authority in a vital, realm. It can lead us up to the threshold of a great experience where we must enter, each man for himself, and that service to the spiritual life is the Bible's inestimable gift.

At the beginning, Christianity was just such a first-hand experience as we have described. The Christian fellowship consisted of a group of men keeping company with Jesus and learning how to live. They had no creeds to recite when they met together; what they believed was still an unstereotyped passion in their hearts. They had no sacraments to distinguish their faith—baptism had been a Jewish rite and even the Lord's Supper was an informal use of bread and wine, the common elements of their daily meal. They had no organizations to join; they never dreamed that the Christian Gospel would build a church outside the synagogue. Christianity in the beginning was an intensely personal experience.

Then the Master went away and the tremendous forces of human life and history laid hold on the movement which so vitally he had begun. His followers began building churches. Just as the Wesleyans had to leave the Church of England, not because they wanted to, but because the Anglicans would not keep them, so the Christians, not because they planned to, but because the synagogue was not large enough to hold them, had to leave the synagogue. They began building creeds; they had to. Every one of the first Christian creeds was written in sheer self-defense. If we had been Christians in those first centuries, when a powerful movement was under way called Gnosticism, which denied that God, the Father Almighty, had made both the heaven and the earth, which said that God had made heaven indeed but that a demigod had made the world, and which denied that Jesus had been born in the flesh and in the flesh had died, we would have done what the first Christians did: we would have defined in a creed what it was the Christians did believe as against that wild conglomeration of Oriental mythology that Gnosticism was, and we would have shouted the creed as a war cry against the Gnostics. That is what the so-called

Apostles' Creed was—the first Christian battle chant, a militant proclamation of the historic faith against the heretics; and every one of its declarations met with a head-on collision some claim of Gnosticism. Then, too, the early Christians drew up rituals; they had to. We cannot keep any spiritual thing in human life, even the spirit of courtesy, as a disembodied wraith. We ritualize it—we bow, we take off our hats, we shake hands, we rise when a lady enters. We have innumerable ways of expressing politeness in a ritual. Neither could they have kept so deep and beautiful a thing as the Christian life without such expression.

So historic Christianity grew, organized, creedalized, ritualized. And ever as it grew, a peril grew with it, for there were multitudes of people who joined these organizations, recited these creeds, observed these rituals, took all the secondary and derived elements of Christianity, but often forgot that vital thing which all this was meant in the first place to express: a first-hand, personal experience of God in Christ. That alone is vital in Christianity; all the rest is once or twice or thrice removed from life. For Christianity is not a creed, nor an organization, nor a ritual. These are important but they are secondary. They are the leaves, not the roots; they are the wires, not the message. Christianity itself is a life.

If, however, Christianity is thus a life, we cannot stereotype its expressions in set and final forms. If it is a life in fellowship with the living God, it will think new thoughts, build new organizations, expand into new symbolic expressions. We cannot at any given time write "finis" after its development. We can no more "keep the faith" by stopping its growth than we can keep a son by insisting on his being forever a child. The progressiveness of Christianity is not simply its response to a progressive age; the progressiveness of Christianity springs from its own inherent vitality. So far is this from being regrettable, that a modern Christian rejoices in it and gladly recognizes not only that he is thinking thoughts and undertaking enterprises which his fathers would not have understood, but also that his children after him will differ quite as much in teaching and practice from the modernity of to-day. It has been the fashion to regard this changeableness with wistful regret. So Wordsworth sings in his sonnet on Mutability:

"Truth fails not; but her outward forms that bear

The longest date do melt like frosty rime,

That in the morning whitened hill and plain

And is no more; drop like the tower sublime

Of yesterday, which royally did wear

Its crown of weeds, but could not even sustain

Some casual shout that broke the silent air,

Or the unimaginable touch of Time."

Such wistfulness, however, while a natural sentiment, is not true to the best Christian thought of our day. He who believes in the living God, while he will be far from calling all change progress, and while he will, according to his judgment, withstand perverse changes with all his might, will also regard the cessation of change as the greatest calamity that could befall religion. Stagnation in thought or enterprise means death for Christianity as certainly as it does for any other vital movement. Stagnation, not change, is Christianity's most deadly enemy, for this is a progressive world, and in a progressive world no doom is more certain than that which awaits whatever is belated, obscurantist and reactionary.

LECTURE V
THE PERILS OF PROGRESS
I

In the history of human thought and social organization there is an interesting pendular swing between conflicting ideas so that, about the time we wake up to recognize that thought is swinging one way, we may be fairly sure that soon it will be swinging the other. Man's social organization, for example, has moved back and forth between the two poles of individual liberty and social solidarity. To pick up the swing of that pendulum only in recent times, we note that out of the social solidarity of the feudal system man swung over to the individual liberty of the free cities; then from the individual liberty of the free cities to the social solidarity of the absolute monarchies; then back again into the individual liberty of the democratic states. We see that now we are clearly swinging over to some new form of social solidarity, of which tendency federalism and socialism are expressions, and doubtless from that we shall recoil toward individual liberty once more. It is a safe generalization that whenever human thought shows some decided trend, a corrective movement is not far away. However enthusiastic we may be, therefore, about the idea of progress and the positive contributions which it can make to our understanding and mastery of life, we may be certain that there are in it the faults of its qualities. If we take it without salt, our children will rise up, not to applaud our far-seeing wisdom, but to blame our easy-going credulity. We have already seen that the very idea of progress sprang up in recent times in consequence of a few factors which predisposed men's minds to social hopefulness. Fortunately, some of these factors, such as the scientific control of life through the knowledge of law, seem permanent, and we are confident that the idea of progress will have abiding meaning for human thought and life. But no study of the matter could be complete without an endeavour to discern the perils in this modern mode of thought and to guard ourselves against accepting as an unmixed blessing what is certainly, like all things human, a blend of good and evil.

One peril involved in the popular acceptance of the idea of progress has been the creation of a superficial, ill-considered optimism which has largely lost sight of the terrific obstacles in human nature against which any real moral advance on earth must win its way. Too often we have taken for granted what a recent book calls "a goal of racial perfection and nobility the splendour of which it is beyond our powers to conceive," and we have dreamed about this earthly paradise like a saint having visions of heaven and counting it as won already because he is predestined to obtain it. Belief in inevitable progress has thus acted as an opiate on many minds, lulling them into an elysium where all things come by wishing and where human ignorance and folly, cruelty and selfishness do not impede the peaceful flowing of their dreams. In a word, the idea of progress has blanketed the sense of sin. Lord Morley spoke once of "that horrid burden and impediment upon the soul which the Churches call Sin, and which, by whatever name you call it, is a real catastrophe in the moral nature of man." The modern age, busy with slick, swift schemes for progress, has too largely lost sight of that.

Indeed, at no point do modern Christians differ more sharply from their predecessors than in the serious facing of the problem of sin. Christians of former times were burdened with a heavy sense of their transgressions, and their primary interest in the Gospel was its promised reestablishment of their guilty souls in the fellowship of a holy God. Modern Christianity, however, is distinguished from all that by a jaunty sense of moral well-being; when we admit our sins we do it with complacency and cheerfulness; our religion is generally characterized by an easy-going self-righteousness. Bunyan's Pilgrim with his lamentable load upon his back, crying, "What shall I do! . . . I am . . . undone by reason of a burden that lieth hard upon me," is no fit symbol of a typically modern Christian.

Doubtless we have cause to be thankful for this swing away from the morbid extremes to which our fathers often went in their sense of sin. It is hard to forgive Jonathan Edwards when one reads in his famous Enfield sermon: "The God that holds you over the pit of hell, much as one holds a spider, or some loathsome insect, over the fire, abhors you, and is dreadfully provoked; . . . you are ten thousand times so abominable in his eyes, as the most hateful and venomous serpent is in ours." Any one who understands human nature could have told him that, after such a black exaggeration of human depravity as he and his generation were guilty of, the Christian movement was foredoomed to swing away over to the opposite extreme of complacent self-righteousness. Unquestionably we have made the swing. In spite of the debacle of the Great War, this is one of the most unrepentant generations that ever walked the earth, dreaming still of automatic progress toward an earthly paradise.

Many factors have gone into the making of this modern mood of self-complacency. New knowledge has helped, by which disasters, such as once awakened our fathers' poignant sense of sin, are now attributed to scientific causes rather than to human guilt. When famines or pestilences came, our fathers thought them God's punishment for sin. When earthquakes shook the earth or comets hung threateningly in the sky, our fathers saw in them a divine demand for human penitence. Such events, referred now to their scientific causes, do not quicken in us a sense of sin. New democracy also has helped in this development of self-complacency. Under autocratic kings the common people were common people and they knew it well. Their dependent commonality was enforced on them by the constant pressure of their social life. Accustomed to call themselves miserable worms before an earthly king, they had no qualms about so estimating themselves before the King of Heaven. Democracy, however, elevates us into self-esteem. The genius of democracy is to believe in men, their worth, their possibilities, their capacities for self-direction. Once the dominant political ideas depressed men into self-contempt; now they lift men into self-exaltation. New excuses for sin have aided in creating our mood of self-content. We know more than our fathers did about the effect of heredity and environment on character, and we see more clearly that some souls are not born but damned into the world. Criminals, in consequence, have come not to be so much condemned as pitied, their perversion of character is regarded not so much in terms of iniquity as of disease, and as we thus condone transgression in others, so in ourselves we palliate our wrong. We regard it as the unfortunate but hardly blamable consequence of temperament or training. Our fathers, who thought that the trouble was the devil in them, used to deal sternly with themselves. Like Chinese Gordon, fighting a besetting sin in private prayer, they used to come out from their inward struggles saying, "I hewed Agag in pieces before the Lord." But we are softer with ourselves; we find in lack of eugenics or in cruel circumstance a good excuse.

Undoubtedly, the new theology has helped to encourage this modern mood of self-complacency. Jonathan Edwards' Enfield sermon pictured sinners held over the blazing abyss of hell in the hands of a wrathful deity who at any moment was likely to let go, and so terrific was that discourse in its delivery that women fainted and strong men clung in agony to the pillars of the church. Obviously, we do not believe in that kind of God any more, and as always in reaction we swing to the opposite extreme, so in the theology of these recent years we have taught a very mild, benignant sort of deity. One of our popular drinking songs sums up this aspect of our new theology:

"God is not censorious

When His children have their fling."

Indeed, the god of the new theology has not seemed to care acutely about sin; certainly he has not been warranted to punish heavily; he has been an indulgent parent and when we have sinned, a polite "Excuse me" has seemed more than adequate to make amends. John Muir, the naturalist, was accustomed during earthquake shocks in California to assuage the anxieties of perturbed Eastern visitors by saying that it was only Mother Earth trotting her children on her knee. Such poetizing is quite in the style of the new theology. Nevertheless, the description, however pretty, is not an adequate account of a real earthquake, and in this moral universe there are real earthquakes, as this generation above all others ought to know, when man's sin, his greed, his selfishness, his rapacity roll up across the years an accumulating mass of consequence until at last in a mad collapse the whole earth crashes into ruin. The moral order of the world has not been trotting us on her knees these recent years; the moral order of the world has been dipping us in hell; and because the new theology had not been taking account of such possibilities, had never learned to preach on that text in the New Testament, "It is a fearful thing to fall into the hands of the living God," we were ill prepared for the experience.

Many factors like those which we have named have contributed to create our modern negligence of the problem of sin, but under all of them and permeating them has been the idea that automatic progress is inherent in the universe. This evolving cosmos has been pictured as a fool-proof world where men could make and love their lies, with their souls dead and their stomachs well alive, with selfish profit the motive of their economic order and narrow nationalism the slogan of their patriotism, and where still, escaping the consequences, they could live in a progressive society. A recent writer considers it possible that "over the crest of the hill the Promised Land stretches away to the far horizons smiling in eternal sunshine." The picture is nonsense. All the progress this world ever will know waits upon the conquest of sin. Strange as it may sound to the ears of this modern age, long tickled by the amiable idiocies of evolution popularly misinterpreted, this generation's deepest need is not these dithyrambic songs about inevitable progress, but a fresh sense of personal and social sin.

What the scientific doctrine of evolution really implies is something much more weighty and sinister than frothy optimism. When a preacher now quotes Paul, "as in Adam all die," not many of the younger generation understand him, but when we are told that we came out of low, sub-human beginnings, that we carry with us yet the bestial leftovers of an animal heritage to be fought against and overcome and left behind, well-instructed members of this generation ought to comprehend. Yet in saying that, we are dealing with the same fundamental fact which Paul was facing when he said, "as in Adam all die"; we are handling the same unescapable experience out of which the old doctrine of original sin first came; we are facing a truth which it will not pay us to forget: that humanity's sinful nature is not something which you and I alone make up by individual deeds of wrong, but that it is an inherited mortgage and handicap on the whole human family. Why is it that if we let a field run wild it goes to weeds, while if we wish wheat we must fight for every grain of it? Why is it that if we let human nature run loose it goes to evil, while he who would be virtuous must struggle to achieve character? It is because, in spite of our optimisms and evasions, that fact still is here, which our fathers often appraised more truly than we, that human nature, with all its magnificent possibilities, is like the earth's soil filled with age-long seeds and roots of evil growth, and that progress in goodness, whether personal or social, must be achieved by grace of some power which can give us the victory over our evil nature.

In past generations it was the preachers who talked most about sin and thundered against it from their pulpits, but now for years they have been very reticent about it. Others, however, have not been still. Scientists have made us feel the ancient heritage that must be fought against; novelists have written no great novel that does not swirl around some central sin; the work of the dramatists from Shakespeare until Ibsen is centrally concerned with the problem of human evil; and now the psycho-analysts are digging down into the unremembered thoughts of men to bring up into the light of day the origins of our spiritual miseries in frustrated and suppressed desire. We do not need artificially to conjure up a sense of sin. All we need to do is to open our eyes to facts. Take one swift glance at the social state of the world to-day. Consider our desperate endeavours to save this rocking civilization from the consequences of the blow just delivered it by men's iniquities. That should be sufficient to indicate that this is no fool-proof universe automatically progressive, but that moral evil is still the central problem of mankind.

One would almost say that the first rule for all who believe in a progressive world is not to believe in it too much. Long ago Plato said that he drove two horses, one white and tractable, the other black and fractious; Jesus said that two masters sought man's allegiance, one God, the other mammon; Paul said that his soul was the battle-ground of two forces, one of which he called spirit and the other flesh; and only the other day one of our own number told of the same struggle between two men in each of us, one Dr. Jekyll, the other Mr. Hyde. That conflict still is pivotal in human history. The idea of progress can defeat itself no more surely than by getting itself so believed that men expect automatic social advance apart from the conquest of personal and social sin.

II

Another result of our superficial confidence in the idea of progress is reliance upon social palliatives instead of radical cures for our public maladies. We are so predisposed to think that the world inherently wants to be better, is inwardly straining to be better, that we are easily fooled into supposing that some slight easement of external circumstance will at once release the progressive forces of mankind and save the race. When, for example, one compares the immense amount of optimistic expectancy about a warless world with the small amount of radical thinking as to what really is the matter with us, he may well be amazed at the unfounded regnancy of the idea of progress. We rejoice over some slight disarmament as though that were the cure of our international shame, whereas always one can better trust a real Quaker with a gun than a thug without one. So the needs of our international situation, involving external disarmament, to be sure, involve also regenerations of thought and spirit much more radical than any rearrangement of outward circumstance. To forget that is to lose the possibility of real progress; and insight into these deep-seated needs is often dimmed by our too amiable and innocent belief in automatic social advance waiting to take place on the slightest excuse.

To take but a single illustration of a radical change in men's thinking, difficult to achieve and yet indispensable to a decent world, consider the group of prejudices and passions which center about nationalism and which impede the real progress of international fraternity. What if all Christians took Jesus in earnest in his attitude that only one object on earth is worthy of the absolute devotion of a man—the will of God for all mankind—and that therefore no nationality nor patriotism whatsoever should be the highest object of man's loyalty? That ought to be an axiom to us, who stood with the Allies against Germany. Certainly, we condemned Germany roundly enough because so many of her teachers exalted the state as an object of absolute loyalty. When in Japan one sees certain classes of people regarding the Mikado as divine and rating loyalty to him as their highest duty, it is easy to condemn that. When, however, a man says in plain English: I am an American but I am a Christian first and I am an American only in the sense in which I can be an American, being first of all a Christian, and my loyalty to America does not begin to compare with my superior loyalty to God's will for all mankind and, if ever national action makes these two things conflict, I must choose God and not America – to the ears of many that plain statement has a tang of newness and danger. In the background of even Christian minds, Jesus to the contrary notwithstanding, one finds the tacit assumption, counted almost too sacred to be examined, that of course a man's first loyalty is to his nation.

Indeed, we Protestants ought to feel a special responsibility for this nationalism that so takes the place of God. In medieval and Catholic Europe folk did not so think of nationalism. Folk in medieval Europe were taught that their highest obligation was to God or, as they would have phrased it, to the Church; that the Church could at any time dispense them from any obligation to king or nation; that the Church could even make the king, the symbol of the nation, stand three days in the snow outside the Pope's door at Canossa. Every boy and girl in medieval Europe was taught that his first duty was spiritual and that no nationality nor patriotism could compare with that. Then we Protestants began our battle for spiritual liberty against the tyranny of Rome, and as one of the most potent agencies in the winning of our battle we helped to develop the spirit of nationality. In place of the Holy Roman Church we put state churches. In place of devotion to the Vatican we were tempted to put devotion to the nation. Luther did more than write spiritual treatises; he sent out ringing, patriotic appeals to the German nobility against Rome. It is not an accident that absolute nationalism came to its climacteric in Germany where Protestantism began. For Protestantism, without ever intending it, as an unexpected by-product of its fight for spiritual liberty, helped to break up western Europe into nations, where nationalism absorbed the loyalty of the people. And now that little tiger cub we helped to rear has become a great beast and its roaring shakes the earth.

A superficial confidence in automatic progress, therefore, which neglects an elemental fact like this at the root of our whole international problem is futile; it leads nowhere; it is rose water prescribed for leprosy. The trouble with nationalism is profound and this is the gist of it: we may be unselfish personally, but we group ourselves into social units called nations, where we, being individually unselfish with reference to the group, are satisfied with ourselves, but where all the time the group itself is not unselfish, but, it may be, is aggressively and violently avaricious. Yet to most people our sacrificial loyalty to the nation would pass for virtue, even though the nation as a whole were exploiting its neighbours or waging a useless, unjust war. The loyalty of Germans to Germany may be rated as the loftiest goodness no matter what Germany as a whole is doing, and the loyalty of Americans to America may be praised as the very passport to heaven while America as a whole may be engaged in a nationally unworthy enterprise. The fine spirit of men's devotion within the limits of the group disguises the ultimate selfishness of the whole procedure and cloaks a huge sin under a comparatively small unselfishness.

We can see that same principle at work in our industrial situation. We break up into two groups; we are trades unionists or associated employers. We are unselfish so far as our group is concerned; we make it a point of honour to support our economic class; it is part of our code of duty to be loyal there. But while we are thus unselfish with reference to the group, the group itself is not unselfish; the group itself is fighting a bitter and selfish conflict, avaricious and often cruel. There is no ultimate way out of this situation which does not include the activity of people who have a loyalty that is greater than their groups. Henry George was once introduced at Cooper Institute, New York City, by a chairman who, wishing to curry favour with the crowd, called out with a loud voice, "Henry George, the friend of the workingman." George stood up and sternly began, "I am not the friend of the workingman"; then after a strained silence, "and I am not the friend of the capitalist"; then after another silence, "I am for men; men simply as men, regardless of any accidental or superficial distinctions of race, creed, colour, class, or yet function or employment." Until we can get that larger loyalty into the hearts of men, all the committees on earth cannot solve our industrial problems.

Nor can anything else make it possible to solve our international problem. The curse of nationalism is that, having pooled the unselfishness of persons in one group under one national name and of persons in another group under another national name, it uses this beautiful unselfishness of patriotism to carry out national enterprises that are fundamentally selfish. One element, therefore, is indispensable in any solution: enough Christians, whether they call themselves by that name or not, who have caught Jesus' point of view that only one loyalty on earth is absolute – the will of God for all mankind. This last summer I spent one Sunday night in the home of Mr. Ozaki, perhaps the leading liberal of Japan, a man who stands in danger of assassination any day for his international attitude. Suddenly he turned on me and said, "If the United States should go into a war which you regarded as unjust and wrong, what would you do?" I had to answer him swiftly and I had to give him the only answer that a Christian minister could give and keep his self-respect. I said, "If the United States goes into a war which I think is unjust and wrong, I will go into my pulpit the next Sunday morning and in the name of God denounce that war and take the consequence." Surely, a man does not have to be a theoretical pacifist, which I am not, to see how indispensable that attitude is to a Christian. There is hardly anything more needed now in the international situation than a multitude of people who will sit in radical judgment on the actions of their governments, so that when the governments of the world begin to talk war they will know that surely they must face a mass of people rising up to say: War? Why war? We are no longer dumb beasts to be led to the slaughter; we no longer think that any state on earth is God Almighty. If, however, we are to have that attitude strong enough so that it will stand the strain of mob psychology and the fear of consequences, it must be founded deep, as was Jesus' attitude: one absolute loyalty to the will of God for all mankind. So far from hurting true patriotism, this attitude would be the making of patriotism. It would purge patriotism from all its peril, would exalt it, purify it, make of it a blessing, not a curse. But whatever be the effect upon patriotism, the Christian is committed by the Master to a prior loyalty; he is a citizen of the Kingdom of God in all the earth.

An easy-going belief in inherent and inevitable progress, therefore, is positively perilous in the manifoldly complex social situation, from which only the most careful thinking and the most courageous living will ever rescue us. The Christian Church is indeed entrusted, in the message of Jesus, with the basic principles of life which the world needs, but the clarity of vision which sees their meaning and the courage of heart which will apply them are not easy to achieve. Some of us have felt that acutely these last few years; all of us should have learned that whatever progress is wrought out upon this planet will be sternly fought for and hardly won. Belief in the idea of progress does not mean that this earth is predestined to drift into Paradise like thistledown before an inevitable wind.

III

A third peril associated with the idea of progress is quite as widespread as the other two and in some ways more insidious. The idea is prevalent that progress involves the constant supersession of the old by the new so that we, who have appeared thus late in human history and are therefore the heirs "of all the ages, in the foremost files of time," may at once assume our superiority to the ancients. The modern man, living in a world supposedly progressing from early crude conditions toward perfection, has shifted the golden age from the past to the future, and in so doing has placed himself in much closer proximity to it than his ancestors were. The world is getting better — such is the common assumption which is naturally associated with the idea of progress. As one enthusiastic sponsor of this proposition puts it:

"Go back ten years, and there was no airship; fifteen years, and there was no wireless telegraphy; twenty-five years, and there was no automobile; forty years, and there was no telephone, and no electric light; sixty years, and there was no photograph, and no sewing machine; seventy-five years, no telegraph; one hundred years, no railway and no steamship; one hundred and twenty-five years, no steam engine; two hundred years, no post-office; three hundred years, no newspaper; five hundred years, no printing press; one thousand years, no compass, and ships could not go out of sight of land; two thousand years, no writing paper, but parchments of skin and tablets of wax and clay. Go back far enough and there were no plows, no tools, no iron, no cloth; people ate acorns and roots and lived in caves and went naked or clothed themselves in the skins of wild beasts."

Such is the picture of human history upon this planet which occupies the modern mind, and one implication often drawn is that we have outgrown the ancients and that they might well learn from us and not we from them.

Christians, however, center their allegiance around ideas and personalities which are, from the modern standpoint, very old indeed. The truths that were wrought out in the developing life and faith of the Hebrew-Christian people are still the regulative Christian truths, and the personality who crowned the whole development is still the Christians' Lord. They are challenged, however, to maintain this in a progressive world. Men do not think of harking back to ancient Palestine nineteen centuries ago for their business methods, their educational systems, their scientific opinions, or anything else in ordinary life whatever. Then why go back to ancient Palestine for the chief exemplar of the spiritual life? This is a familiar modern question which springs directly from popular interpretations of progress.

"Dim tracts of time divide

  Those golden days from me;

Thy voice comes strange o'er years of change;

  How can I follow Thee?

"Comes faint and far Thy voice

  From vales of Galilee;

Thy vision fades in ancient shades;

  How should we follow Thee?"

Behind this familiar mood lies one of the most significant changes that has ever passed over the human mind. The medieval age was tempted to look backward for its knowledge of everything. Philosophy was to be found in Aristotle, science in Pliny and his like. It was the ancients who were wise; it was the ancients who had understood nature and had known God. The farther back you went the nearer you came to the venerable and the authoritative. As, therefore, in every other realm folk looked back for knowledge, so it was most natural that they should look back for their religion, too. To find philosophy in Aristotle and to find spiritual life in Christ required not even the turning of the head. In all realms the age in its search for knowledge was facing backwards. It was a significant hour in the history of human thought when that attitude began to give way. The scandal caused by Alessandro Tassoni's attacks on Homer and Aristotle in the early seventeenth century resounded through Europe. He advanced the new and astonishing idea that, so far from having degenerated since ancient times, the race had advanced and that the moderns were better than their sires. This new idea prevailed as belief in progress grew. It met, however, with violent opposition, and the remnants of that old controversy are still to be found in volumes like George Hakewill's five hundred page folio published in 1627 on "the common errour touching Nature's perpetuall and universall decay." But from the seventeenth century on the idea gained swift ascendency that the human race, like an individual, is growing up, that humanity is becoming wiser with the years, that we can know more than Aristotle and Pliny, that we should look, not back to the ancients, but rather to ourselves and to our offspring, for the real wisdom which maturity achieves. Once what was old seemed wise and established; what was new seemed extempore and insecure: now what is old seems outgrown; what is new seems probable and convincing. Such is the natural and prevalent attitude in a world where the idea of progress is in control. Nor can the applications of this idea to the realm of religion be evaded. If we would not turn back to Palestine nineteen centuries ago for anything else, why should we turn back to find there the Master of our spiritual life? In a word, our modern belief in progress, popularly interpreted, leads multitudes of people to listen with itching ears for every new thing, while they condescend to all that is old in religion, and in particular conclude that, while Jesus lived a wonderful life for his own day, that was a long time ago and surely we must be outgrowing him.

That this attitude is critically perilous to the integrity of the Christian movement will at once be obvious to any one whose own spiritual experience is centered in Christ. From the beginning until now the faith of Christian people has been primarily directed, not to a set of abstract principles, nor to a set of creedal definitions, but to a Person. Christians have been people believing in Jesus Christ. This abiding element has put unity into Christian history. The stream of Christian thought and progress has never been twice the same, yet for all that it has been a continuous stream and not an aimless, sprawling flood, and this unity and consistency have existed for one reason chiefly: the influence of the personality of Jesus. Folk may have been Romanists or Protestants, ritualists or Quakers, reactionaries or progressives, but still they have believed in Jesus. His personality has been the sun around which even in their differences they have swung like planets in varying orbits. Take the personality of Jesus out of Christian history and what you have left is chaos.

Moreover, it is the personality of Jesus that has been the source of Christianity's transforming influence on character. Ask whence has come that power over the spirits of men which we recognize as Christianity at its mightiest and best, and the origin must be sought, not primarily in our theologies or rubrics or churches, but in the character and spirit of Jesus. He himself is the central productive source of power in Christianity. We have come so to take this for granted that we do not half appreciate the wonder of it. This personality, who so has mastered men, was born sixty generations ago in a small village in an outlying Roman province, and until he was thirty years of age he lived and worked as a carpenter among his fellow townsfolk, attracting no wide consideration. Then for three years or less he poured out his life in courageous teaching and sacrificial service, amid the growing hatred and hostility of his countrymen, until he was put to death by crucifixion "because he stirred up the people." Anatole France, in one of his stories, represents Pilate in his later years as trying to remember the trial and death of Jesus and being barely able to recall it. That incident had been so much a part of the day's work in governing a province like Judea that it had all but escaped his recollection. Such a representation of the case is not improbable. It is easy so to tell the story of

Jesus' life as to make his continued influence seem incredible. None would have supposed that nineteen centuries after his death, Lecky, the historian of European morals, would say, "The simple record of three short years of active life has done more to regenerate and to soften mankind than all the disquisitions of philosophers, and all the exhortations of moralists." None would have thought that sixty generations after he was gone, Montefiori, a Jew, putting his finger on the source of Christianity's power, would light upon the phrase "For the sake of Jesus," and would cry: "Of what fine lives and deaths has not this motive been the spring and the sustainment!" None would have thought that so long after Calvary seemed to end forever the power of Jesus, one of the race's greatest men, David Livingstone, engaged in one of the race's most courageous enterprises, breaking his way into the untraveled jungles of Africa, would sing as he went, for so his journal says he did,

"Jesus, the very thought of Thee

With sweetness fills my breast"?

Take the personality of the Master out of Christian history and we have robbed it of its central moral power.

Moreover, the personality of Jesus has always been the standard of reformation when Christianity has become recreant or laggard or corrupt. A man named John Wilkes started a political movement in England in the eighteenth century, and around him sprang up a party who called themselves Wilkites. These followers of Wilkes, however, went to extremes so wild and perilous that poor John Wilkes himself had to explain to everybody that, as for him, he was not a Wilkite. This lapse of a movement from the original intention of its founder is familiar in history and nowhere is it more clearly illustrated than in Christianity. The Master, watching Western Christendom today, with all our hatred, bitterness, war, would have to say, If this is Christianity, then I am not a Christian. The Master, wandering through our cathedrals with their masses, waxen images and votive gifts, or through our Protestant churches with their fine-spun speculations insisted on as necessary to belief if one is to be a child of grace, would have to say, If this is Christianity, then I am not a Christian. Indeed, just this sort of service the Master always has been rendering his movement; he is the perennial rebuke of all that is degenerate and false in Christianity. Whenever reform has come, whenever real Christianity has sprung up again through the false and superficial, the movement has been associated with somebody's rediscovery of Jesus Christ. Saint Francis of Assisi rediscovered him, and made a spot of spiritual beauty at the heart of the medieval age. John Wesley rediscovered him and his compassion for the outcast, and led the Church into a new day of evangelism and philanthropy. William Carey rediscovered him and his unbounded care for men, and blazed the trail for a new era of expansive Christianity. And if today many of us are deeply in earnest about the application of Christian principles to the social life of men, it is because we have rediscovered him and the spirit of his Good Samaritan. In an old myth, Antaeus, the child of Earth, could be overcome when he was lifted from contact with the ground but, whenever he touched again the earth from which he sprang, his old power came back once more. Such is Christianity's relation with Jesus Christ. If, therefore, the idea of progress involves the modern man's condescension to the Master as the outgrown seer of an ancient day, the idea of progress has given Christianity an incurable wound.

Before we surrender to such a popular interpretation of the meaning of progress, we may well discriminate between two aspects of human life in one of which we plainly have progressed, but in the other of which progress is not so evident. In the Coliseum in ancient Rome centuries ago, a group of Christians waited in the arena to be devoured by the lions, and eighty thousand spectators watched their vigil. Those Christians were plain folk—"not many mighty, not many noble"—and every one of them could have escaped that brutal fate if he had been willing to burn a little incense to the Emperor. Turn now to ourselves, eighteen hundred years afterwards. We have had a long time to outgrow the character and fidelity of those first Christians; do we think that we have done so? As we imagine ourselves in their places, are we ready with any glibness to talk about progress in character? Those first Christians never had ridden in a trolley car; they never had seen a subway; they never had been to a moving picture show; they never had talked over a telephone. There are innumerable ways in which we have progressed far beyond them. But character, fidelity, loyalty to conscience and to God — are we sure of progress there?

To hear some people talk, one would suppose that progress is simply a matter of chronology. That one man or generation comes in time after another is taken as sufficient evidence that the latter has of course superseded the earlier. Do we mean that because Tennyson came after Shelly he is therefore the greater poet? What has chronology to do with spiritual quality and creativeness, which always must rise from within, out of the abysmal depths of personality? Professor Gilbert Murray, thinking primarily in a realm outside religion altogether, chastises this cheap and superficial claim of advance in spiritual life:

"As to Progress, it is no doubt a real fact. To many of us it is a truth that lies somewhere near the roots of our religion. But it is never a straight march forward; it is never a result that happens of its own accord. It is only a name for the mass of accumulated human effort, successful here, baffled there, misdirected and driven astray in a third region, but on the whole and in the main producing some cumulative result. I believe this difficulty about Progress, this fear that in studying the great teachers of the past we are in some sense wantonly sitting at the feet of savages, causes real trouble of mind to many keen students. The full answer to it would take us beyond the limits of this paper and beyond my own range of knowledge. But the main lines of the answer seem to me clear. There are in life two elements, one transitory and progressive, the other comparatively if not absolutely non-progressive and eternal, and the soul of man is chiefly concerned with the second. Try to compare our inventions, our material civilization, our stores of accumulated knowledge, with those of the age of Aeschylus or Aristotle or St. Francis, and the comparison is absurd. Our superiority is beyond question and beyond measure. But compare any chosen poet of our age with Aeschylus, any philosopher with Aristotle, any saintly preacher with St. Francis, and the result is totally different. I do not wish to argue that we have fallen below the standard of those past ages; but it is clear that we are not definitely above them. The things of the spirit depend on will, on effort, on aspiration, on the quality of the individual soul, and not on discoveries and material advances which can be accumulated and added up."

Let any Christian preacher test out this matter and discover for himself its truth. We are preachers of the Gospel in the twentieth century. St. Francis of Assisi was a preacher of the Gospel in the thirteenth century. We know many things which St. Francis and his generation never could have known but, when we step back through that outward change into the spirit of St. Francis himself, we must take the shoes from off our feet, for the place whereon we stand is holy ground. We may not talk in such an hour about progress in Christian character in terms of chronology, for a modern minister might well pray to touch the garment's hem of such a spirit as St. Francis had! When, then, one speaks of outgrowing Jesus, one would do well to get a better reason than simply the fact that he was born nineteen centuries ago. The truth is that humanity has been upon this planet hundreds of thousands of years, while our known history reaches back, and that very dimly, through only some four or five thousand. In that known time there has certainly been no biological development in man that any scientist has yet discerned. Even the brain of man in the ice age was apparently as large as ours. Moreover, within that period of history well known to us, we can see many ups and downs of spiritual life, mountain peaks of achievement in literature and art and religion, with deep valleys intervening, but we cannot be sure that the mountain peaks now are higher than they used to be. The art of the two centuries culminating about 1530 represents a glorious flowering of creative genius, but it was succeeded by over three centuries of descent to the abominations of ugliness which the late eighteenth century produced. We have climbed up a little since then, but not within distant reach of those lovers and makers of beauty from whose hearts and hands the Gothic cathedrals came. Progress in history has lain in the power of man to remember and so to accumulate for general use the discoveries, both material and ethical, of many individuals; it has lain in man's increasing information about the universe, in his increasing mastery over external nature, and in the growing integration of his social life; it has not lain in the production of creative personalities appearing in the course of history with ever greater sublimity of spirit and grasp of intellect. Where is there a mind on earth today like Plato's? Where is there a spirit today like Paul's?

The past invites us still to look back for revelations in the realm of creative personality. Some things have been done in history, like the sculptures of Phidias, that never have been done so well since and that perhaps never will be done so well again. As for the Bible, we may well look back to that. There is no book to compare with it in the realm of religion. Most of the books we read are like the rainwater that fell last night, a superficial matter, soon running off. But the Bible is a whole sea—the accumulated spiritual gains of ages—and to know it and to love it, to go down beside it and dip into it, to feel its vast expanse, the currents that run through it, and the tides that lift it, is one of the choicest and most rewarding spiritual privileges that we enjoy. As for Jesus, it is difficult to see what this twentieth century can mean by supposing that it has outgrown him. It has outgrown countless elements in his generation and many forms of thought which he shared with his generation, but it never will outgrow his spirit, his faith in God, his principles of life: "Our Father who art in heaven, Hallowed by thy name;" "Thou shalt love the Lord thy God with all thy heart, and with all thy soul, and with all thy strength, and with all thy mind; and thy neighbor as thyself;" "It is not the will of your Father who is in heaven, that one of these little ones should perish;" "By this shall all men know that ye are my disciples, if ye have love one to another;" "If any man would be first, he shall be last of all, and servant of all;" "All things therefore whatsoever ye would that men should do unto you, even so do ye also unto them;" "Love your enemies, and pray for them that persecute you;" "Thy will be done, as in heaven, so on earth." Take principles like these, set them afire in a flaming life the like of which has never come to earth, and we have in Jesus a revelation of the spiritual world which is not going to be outgrown. Still for the Christian he is Saviour and Lord, and across the centuries in his face shines the light of the knowledge of the glory of God.

Progress, therefore, intelligently apprehended, does not involve that flippant irreverence for the past that so often is associated with it. It offers no encouragement to the chase after vagaries in which so many moderns indulge, as though all that is old were belated and all that is novel were true. The idea of progress has led more than one eager mind to think that the old religions were outgrown; that they were the belated leftovers of a bygone age and were not for modern minds; that a new religion fitted to our new needs alone would do. Suppose, however, that one should say: The English language is an archaic affair; it has grown like Topsy, by chance; it has carried along with it the forms of thinking of outgrown generations; it is not scientific; what we need is a new language built to order to meet our wants. In answer one must acknowledge that the English language is open to very serious criticism, that one can never tell from the way a word is spelled how it is going to be pronounced, nor from the way it is pronounced how it is going to be spelled. One must agree that the English language makes one phrase do duty for many different meanings. When two people quarrel, they make up; before the actor goes upon the stage, he makes up; the preacher goes into his study to make up his sermon; when we do wrong we try to make up for it; and the saucy lad in school behind his teacher's back makes up a face. The English language is fearfully and wonderfully made. But merely because the English language has such ungainly developments, we are not likely to surrender it and adopt instead a modern language made to order, like Esperanto. Say what one will about English, it is the speech in which our poets have sung and our prophets have prophesied and our seers have dreamed dreams. If any do not like it they may get a new one, but most of us will stay where we still can catch the accents of the master spirits who have spoken in our tongue. There are words in the English language that no Esperanto words ever can take the place of: home and honour and love and God, words that have been sung about and prayed over and fought for by our sires for centuries, and that come to us across the ages with accumulated meanings, like caskets full of jewels. Surely we are not going to give up the English language. Progress does not mean surrendering it, but developing it.

We shall not give up Christianity. It has had ungainly developments; it does need reformation; many elements in it are pitiably belated; but, for all that, the profoundest need of the world is real Christianity, the kind of life the Master came to put into the hearts of men. Progress does not mean breaking away from it, but going deeper into it.

Here, then, are the three perils which tempt the believer in progress: a silly underestimate of the tremendous force of human sin, which withstands all real advance; superficial reliance upon social palliatives to speed the convalescence of the world, when only radical cures will do; flippant irreverence toward the past, when, as a matter of fact, the light we have for the future shines upon us from behind. He who most believes in progress needs most to resist its temptations.

LECTURE VI
PROGRESS AND GOD
I

We may well begin our final lecture, on the interplay between the idea of progress and the idea of God, by noting that only faith in God can satisfy man's craving for spiritual stability amid change. The central element in the conception of a progressive world is that men's thoughts and lives have changed, are changing and will change, that nothing therefore is settled in the sense of being finally formulated, that creation has never said its last word on any subject or landed its last hammer blow on any task. Such an outlook on life, instead of being exhilarating, is to many disquieting in the extreme. In particular it is disquieting in religion, one of whose functions has always been to provide stability, to teach men amid the transient to see the eternal. If in a changing world religious thought changes too, if in that realm also new answers are given to old questions and new questions rise that never have been answered before, if forms of faith in which men once trusted are outgrown, man's unsettlement seems to be complete. The whole world then is like a huge kaleidoscope turning round and round and, as it turns, the manifold elements in human experience, even its religious doctrines and practices, arrange and rearrange themselves in endless permutations. How then in such a world can religion mean to us what it has meant to the saints who of old, amid a shaken world, have sung:

"Change and decay in all around I see;

O Thou, Who changest not, abide with me!"

This fear of the unsettling effects of the idea of progress accounts for most of the resentment against it in the realm of theology, and for the desperate endeavours which perennially are made to congeal the Christian movement at some one stage and to call that stage final. Stability, however, can never be achieved by resort to such reactionary dogmatism. What one obtains by that method is not stability but stagnation, and the two, though often confused, are utterly different. Stagnation is like a pool, stationary, finished, and without progressive prospects. A river, however, has another kind of steadfastness altogether. It is not stationary; it flows; it is never twice the same and its enlarging prospects as it widens and deepens in its course are its glory. Nevertheless, the Hudson and the Mississippi and the Amazon are among the most stable and abiding features which nature knows. They will probably outlast many mountains. They will certainly outlast any pool.

The spiritual stability which we may have in a progressive world is of this latter sort, if we believe in the living God. It is so much more inspiring than the stagnation of the dogmatist that one wonders how any one, seeing both, could choose the inferior article in which to repose his trust. Consider, for example, the development of the idea of God himself, the course of which through the Bible we briefly traced in a previous lecture. From Sinai to Calvary—was ever a record of progressive revelation more plain or more convincing? The development begins with Jehovah disclosed in a thunder-storm on a desert mountain, and it ends with Christ saying: "God is a Spirit: and they that worship him must worship in spirit and truth;" it begins with a war-god leading his partisans to victory and it ends with men saying, "God is love; and he that abideth in love abideth in God, and God abideth in him;" it begins with a provincial deity loving his tribe and hating its enemies and it ends with the God of the whole earth worshiped by "a great multitude, which no man could number, out of every nation and of all tribes and peoples and tongues;" it begins with a God who commands the slaying of the Amalekites, "both man and woman, infant and suckling," and it ends with a Father whose will it is that not "one of these little ones should perish;" it begins with God's people standing afar off from his lightnings and praying that he might not speak to them lest they die and it ends with men going into their inner chambers and, having shut the door, praying to their Father who is in secret. Here is no pool; here is a river, the streams whereof make glad the city of God.

Consider as well the course of the idea of God after the close of the New Testament canon. The Biblical conception of God in terms of righteous and compassionate personal will went out into a world of thought where Greek metaphysics was largely in control. There God was conceived in terms of substance, as the ontological basis and ground of all existence—immutable, inscrutable, unqualified pure being. These two ideas, God as personal will, and God as metaphysical substance, never perfectly coalescing, flowed together. In minds like St. Augustine's one finds them both. God as pure being and God as gracious and righteous personal will—St. Augustine accepted both ideas but never harmonized them. Down through Christian history one can see these two conceptions complementing each other, each balancing the other's eccentricities. The Greek idea runs out toward pantheism in Spinoza and Hegel. The Biblical idea runs out toward deism in Duns Scotus and Calvin. In the eighteenth century an extreme form of deism held the field and God, as personal will, was conceived as the Creator, who in a dim and distant past had made all things. In the nineteenth century the thought of God swung back to terms of immanence, and God, who had been crowded out of his world, came flooding in as the abiding life of all of it.

As one contemplates a line of development like this, he must be aware that, while change is there, it is not aimless, discontinuous, chaotic change. The riverbed in which this stream of thought flows is stable and secure; the whole development is controlled by man's abiding spiritual need of God and God's unceasing search for man. One feels about it as he might about man's varying, developing methods of telling the time of day. Men began by noting roughly the position of the sun or the length of shadows; they went on to make sun-dials, then water-clocks, then sand-glasses; then weight-driven clocks were blunderingly tried and, later, watches, used first as toys, so little were they to be relied upon. The story of man's telling of the time of day is a story of progressive change, but it does not lack stability. The sun and stars and the revolution of the earth abide. The changes in man's telling of the time have been simply the unfolding of an abiding relationship between man and his world.

So the development of man's religious ideas from early, crude beginnings until now is not a process which one would wish to stop at any point in order to achieve infallible security. The movement is not haphazard and discontinuous change, like disparate particles in a kaleidoscope falling together in new but vitally unrelated ways. Upon the contrary, its course is a continuous path which can be traced, recovered in thought, conceived as a whole. We can see where our ideas came from, what now they are, and in what direction they probably will move. The stability is in the process itself, arising out of the abiding relationships of man with the eternal.

Indeed, the endeavour to achieve stability by methods which alone can bring stagnation, the endeavor, that is, to hit upon dogmatic finality in opinion, is of all things in religion probably the most disastrous in its consequence. Until recent times when reform movements invaded Mohammedanism and higher criticism tackled the problem of the Koran, one could see this achievement of stagnation in Islam in all its inglorious success. The Koran was regarded as having been infallibly written, word for word, in heaven before ever it came to earth. The Koran therefore was a book of inerrant and changeless opinion. But the Koran enshrines the best theological and ethical ideas of Arabia at the time when it was written: God was an oriental monarch, ruling in heaven; utter submission to the fate which he decreed was the one law of human relationship with him; and on earth slavery and polygamy and conversion of unbelievers by force were recognized as right. The Koran was ahead of its day, but having been by a theory of inspiration petrified into artificial finality it became the enemy of all opinions which would pass beyond its own.

When, now, one contrasts Mohammedanism with Christianity, one finds an important difference. For all our temptation, succumbed to by multitudes, to make the Bible a Koran, Christianity has had a progressive revelation. In the Bible one can find all the ideas and customs which Mohammedanism has approved and for which it now is hated: its oriental deity decreeing fates, its use of force to destroy unbelievers, its patriarchal polygamy, and its slave systems. All these things, from which we now send missionaries to convert Mohammedans, are in our Bible, but in the Bible they are not final. They are ever being superseded. The revelation is progressive. The idea of God grows from oriental kingship to compassionate fatherhood; the use of force gives way to the appeals of love; polygamy is displaced by monogamy; slavery never openly condemned, even when the New Testament closes, is being underminded by ideas which, like dynamite, in the end will blast to pieces its foundations. We are continually running upon passages like this: "It was said to them of old time, . . . but I say unto you;" "God, having of old time spoken unto the fathers in the prophets by divers portions and in divers manners, hath at the end of these days spoken unto us in his Son;" "The times of ignorance therefore God overlooked; but now he commandeth men that they should all everywhere repent;" and over the doorway out of the New Testament into the Christian centuries that followed is written this inscription: "The spirit of truth . . . shall guide you into all the truth." In a word, finality in the Koran is behind—it lies in the treasured concepts of 600 A. D.—but finality in the Bible is ahead. We are moving toward it. It is too great for us yet to apprehend. Our best thoughts are thrown out in its direction but they do not exhaust its meaning.

"Our little systems have their day;

They have their day and cease to be;

They are but broken lights of thee,

And thou, O Lord, art more than they."

Such is the exultant outlook of a Christian believer on a progressive world. If, however, one is to have this exultant outlook, he must deeply believe in the living God and in the guidance of his Spirit. What irreligion means at this point is not fully understood by most unbelieving folk because most unbelievers do not think through to a conclusion the implications of their own skepticism. We may well be thankful even in the name of religion for a few people like Bertrand Russell. He is not only irreligious but he is intelligently irreligious, and, what is more, he possesses the courage to say frankly and fully what irreligion really means:

"That Man is the product of causes which have no prevision of the end they were achieving; that his origin, his growth, his hopes and fears, his loves and his beliefs, are but the outcome of accidental collocations of atoms; that no fire, no heroism, no intensity of thought and feeling, can preserve an individual life beyond the grave; that all the labours of the ages, all the devotion, all the inspiration, all the noonday brightness of human genius, are destined to extinction in the vast death of the solar system, and that the whole temple of Man's achievement must inevitably be buried beneath the debris of a universe in ruins—all these things, if not quite beyond dispute, are yet so nearly certain, that no philosophy which rejects them can hope to stand. Only within the scaffolding of these truths, only on the firm foundation of unyielding despair, can the soul's habitation henceforth be safely built." Such is the outlook on human life of a frank and thoroughgoing irreligion, and there is nothing exhilarating about it. All progress possible in such a setting is a good deal like a horse-race staged in a theatre, where the horses do indeed run furiously, but where we all know well that they are not getting anywhere. There is a moving floor beneath them, and it is only the shifting of the scenery that makes them seem to go. Is human history like that? Is progress an illusion? Is it all going to end as Bertrand Russell says? Those who believe in the living God are certain of the contrary, for stability amid change is the gift of a progressive, religious faith.

II

It must be evident, however, to any one acquainted with popular ideas of God that if in a progressive world we thus are to maintain a vital confidence in the spiritual nature of creative reality and so rejoice in the guidance of the Spirit amid change, we must win through in our thinking to a very much greater conception of God than that to which popular Christianity has been accustomed. Few passages in Scripture better deserve a preacher's attention than God's accusation against his people in the 50th Psalm: "Thou thoughtest that I was altogether such a one as thyself." The universal applicability of this charge is evident to any one who knows the history of man's religious thought. If in the beginning God did make man in his own image, man has been busy ever since making God in his image, and the deplorable consequences are everywhere to be seen. From idolaters, who bow down before wooden images of the divine in human form, to ourselves, praying to a magnified man throned somewhere in the skies, man has persistently run God into his own mold. To be sure, this tendency of man to think of God as altogether such a one as ourselves is nothing to be surprised at. Even when we deal with our human fellows, we read ourselves into our understandings of them. A contemporary observer tells us that whenever a portrait of Gladstone appeared in French papers he was made to look like a Frenchman, and that when he was represented in Japanese papers his countenance had an unmistakably Japanese cast.

If this habitual tendency to read ourselves into other people is evident even when we deal with human personalities, whom we can know well, how can it be absent from man's thought of the eternal? A man needs only to go out on a starry night with the revelations of modern astronomy in his mind and to consider the one who made all this and whose power sustains it, to see how utterly beyond our adequate comprehension he must be. As men in old tales used to take diffused superhumans, the genii, and by magic word bring them down into a stoppered bottle where they could be held in manageable form, so man has taken the vastness of God and run it into a human symbol.

This persistent anthropomorphism is revealed in our religious ceremonies. Within Christianity itself are systems of priestcraft where the individual believer has no glad, free access to his Father's presence, but where his approach must be mediated by a priestly ritual, his forgiveness assured by a priestly declaration, his salvation sealed by a priestly sacrament. This idea that God must be approached by stated ceremonies came directly from thinking of God in terms of a human monarch. No common man could walk carelessly into the presence of an old-time king. There were proprieties to be observed. There were courtiers who knew the proper approach to royalty, through whom the common folk would better send petitions up and from whom they would better look for favour. So God was pictured as a human monarch with his throne, his scepter, his ministering attendants. Here on earth the priests were those courtiers who knew the effectual way of reaching him, by whom we would best send up our prayers, through whom we would best look for our salvation. Nordau is not exaggerating when he says: "When we have studied the sacrificial rites, the incantations, prayers, hymns, and ceremonies of religion, we have as complete a picture of the relations between our ancestors and their chiefs as if we had seen them with our own eyes."

Our anthropomorphism, however, reaches its most dangerous form in our inward imaginations of God's character. How the pot has called the kettle black! Man has read his vanities into God, until he has supposed that singing anthems to God's praise might flatter him as it would flatter us. Man has read his cruelties into God, and what in moments of vindictiveness and wrath we would like to do our enemies we have supposed Eternal God would do to his. Man has read his religious partisanship into God; he who holds Orion and the Pleiades in his leash, the Almighty and Everlasting God, before whom in the beginning the morning stars sang together, has been conceived as though he were a Baptist or a Methodist, a Presbyterian or an Anglican. Man has read his racial pride into God; nations have thought themselves his chosen people above all his other children because they seemed so to themselves. The centuries are sick with a god made in man's image, and all the time the real God has been saying, "Thou thoughtest that I was altogether such a one as thyself."

The unhappy prevalence of this mental idolatry is one of the chief causes for the loss of religious faith among the younger generation. They have grown up in our homes and churches with their imaginations dwelling on a God made in man's image, and now through education they have moved out into a universe so much too big for that little god of theirs either to have made in the first place or to handle now that they find it hard to believe in him. Astronomers tell us that there are a hundred million luminous stars in our sky, and dark stars in unknown multitudes; that these stars range from a million to ten million miles in diameter; that some of them are so vast that were they brought as close to us as our sun is they would fill the entire horizon; and that these systems are scattered through the stellar spaces at distances so incredible that, were some hardy discoverer to seek our planet in the midst of them, it would be like looking for a needle lost somewhere on the western prairies. The consequence is inevitable: a vast progressive universe plus an inadequate God means that in many minds faith in God goes to pieces.

III

One of the profoundest needs of the Church, therefore, in this new and growing world, is the achievement of such worthy ways of thinking about God and presenting him as will make the very idea of him a help to faith and not a stumbling-block to the faithful. In the attainment of that purpose we need for one thing to approach the thought of God from an angle which to popular Christianity is largely unfamiliar, although it is not unfamiliar in the historic tradition of the Church. Too exclusively have we clung to the mental categories and the resultant phraseology which have grown up around the idea of God as an individual like ourselves. The reasons for the prevalence of this individualized conception of deity are obvious. First, as we have seen, the growth of the idea of God in Hebrew-Christian thought moved out from a very clearly visualized figure on a mountain-top to those expanded and spiritualized forms which glorified the later stages of the Biblical development; and, second, every one of us in his personal religious experience and thought recapitulates the same process, starting as a child with God conceived in very human terms and moving out to expanded and sublimated forms of that childish conception. Whether, then, we consider the source of our idea of God in the Biblical tradition or in our own private experience, we see that it is rooted in and springs up out of a very human conception of him, and that our characteristic words about him, attitudes toward him, and imaginations of him, are associated with these childlike origins. Popular Christianity, therefore, approaches God with the regulative idea of a human individual in its mind, and, while popular Christianity would insist that God is much more than that, it still starts with that, and the enterprise of stretching the conception is only relatively successful. Even when it is successful the result must be a God who is achieved by stretching out a man.

In this situation the only help for many is, for the time being, to leave this endeavour to approach God by way of an expanded and sublimated human individual and to approach God, instead, by way of the Creative

Power from which this amazing universe and all that is within it have arisen. Man's deepest question concerns the nature of the Creative Power from which all things and persons have come. In creation are we dealing with the kind of power which in ordinary life we recognize as physical, or with the kind which we recognize as spiritual? With these two sorts of power we actually deal and, so far as we can see, the ultimate reality which has expressed itself in them must be akin to the one or to the other or to both. He who is convinced that the Creative Power from which all things have come is spiritual believes in God. I have seen that simple statement lift the burden of doubt from minds utterly perplexed and usher befogged spirits out into the liberty of the glory of the children of God. For they did not believe that the Creative Power was dynamic dirt, going it blind; they did believe that the Creative Power was akin to what we know as spirit, but so accustomed were they to the Church's narrower anthropomorphism that they did not suppose that this approach was a legitimate avenue for the soul's faith in God.

Nevertheless, it is a legitimate avenue and in the history of the Church many are the souls that have traveled it. The basis for all mature conceptions of God lies here: that the Power from whom all life proceeds wells up in two forms. One is physical; we can see it, touch it, weigh it, analyze and measure it. The other is spiritual; it is character, conscience, intelligence, purpose, love; we cannot see it, nor touch it, nor weigh it, nor analyze it. We ourselves did not make either of these two expressions of life. They came up together out of the Creative Reality from which we came. When a man thinks of the Power from which all life proceeds, he must say at least this: that when it wells up in us it wells up in two forms and one of them is spirit. How, then, when we think of that Power, can we leave spirit out? At the heart of the eternal is the fountain of that spiritual life which in myself I know.

This thought of God does not start, then, with a magnified man in the heavens; this thought of God starts with the universe itself vibrant with life, tingling with energy, where, when scientists try to analyze matter, they have to trace it back from molecules to atoms, from atoms to electrons, and from electrons to that vague spirituelle thing which they call a "strain in the ether," a universe where there is manifestly no such thing as dead matter, but where everything is alive. When one thinks of the Power that made this, that sustains this, that flows like blood through the veins of this, one cannot easily think that physicalness is enough to predicate concerning him. If the physical adequately could have revealed that Power, there never would have been anything but the physical to reveal him. The fact that spiritual life is here is evidence that it takes spiritual life fully to display the truth about creation's reality. As an old mystic put it: "God sleeps in the stone, he dreams in the animal, he wakes in man!"

It was this approach to God which saved the best spiritual life of the nineteenth century. For in the eighteenth century Christianity came nearer to being driven out of business than ever in her history before. She had believed in a carpenter god who had made the world and occasionally tinkered with it in events which men called miracles. But new knowledge made that carpenter god impossible. Area after area where he had been supposed to operate was closed to him by the discovery of natural law until at last even comets were seen to be law-abiding and he was escorted clean to the edge of the universe and bowed out altogether. Nobody who has not read the contemporary literature of the eighteenth century can know what dryness of soul resulted.

Man, however, cannot live without God. Our fathers had to have God back again. But if God were to come back again he could not return as an occasional tinkerer; he had to come as the life in all that lives, the indwelling presence throughout his creation, whose ways of working are the laws, so that he penetrates and informs them all. No absentee landlord could be welcomed back, but if God came as the resident soul of all creation, men could comprehend that. And he did come back that way. His return is the glory of the nineteenth century. In the best visions of the century's prophets that glory shines.

MRS. BROWNING:

"Earth's crammed with heaven,

And every common bush afire with God:

But only he who sees, takes off his shoes."

TENNYSON:

"Speak to Him, thou, for He hears, and

Spirit with Spirit can meet—

Closer is He than breathing, and nearer

than hands and feet."

COLERIDGE:

"Glory to Thee, Father of Earth and Heaven!

All conscious presence of the Universe!

Nature's vast ever-acting Energy!"

WORDSWORTH:

"a sense sublime

Of something far more deeply interfused,

Whose dwelling is the light of setting suns,

And the round ocean and the living air

And the blue sky, and in the mind of man;

A motion and a spirit, that impels

All thinking things, all objects of all thoughts,

And rolls through all things."

CARLYLE:

"Then sawest thou that this fair Universe, were it in the meanest province thereof, is in very deed the star-domed City of God; that through every star, through every grass-blade, and most through every Living Soul, the glory of a present God still beams. But Nature, which is the Time-vesture of God, and reveals Him to the wise, hides Him from the foolish."

Moreover, this idea of God as the Creative Power conceived in spiritual terms need not lose any of the intimate meanings which have inhered in more personal thoughts of him and which are expressed in the Bible's names for him: Father, Mother, Bridegroom, Husband, Friend. There is indeed this danger in the approach which we have been describing, that we may conceive God as so dispersed everywhere that we cannot find him anywhere and that at last, so diffused, he will lose the practical value on account of which we want him. For we do desire a God who is like ourselves—enough like ourselves so that he can understand us and care for us and enter into our human problems. We do want a human side to God. A man who had seen in Henry Drummond the most beautiful exhibition of God's Spirit that he had ever experienced said that after Henry Drummond died he always prayed up to God by way of Drummond. We make our most vital approaches to God in that way and we always have, from the time we prayed to God through our fathers and mothers until now, when we find God in Christ. We want in God a personality that can answer ours, and we can have it without belittling in the least his greatness.

I know a man who says that one of the turning points of his spiritual experience came on a day when for the first time it dawned on him that he never had seen his mother. Now, his mother was the major molding influence in his life. He could have said about her what Longfellow said in a letter to his mother, written when he was twenty-one. "For me," wrote Longfellow, "a line from my mother is more efficacious than all the homilies preached in Lent; and I find more incitement to virtue in merely looking at your handwriting than in a whole volume of ethics and moral discourses." So this man would have felt about the pervasive influence of his mother. Then it dawned on him one day that he never had seen her. To be sure, he had seen the bodily instrument by which she had been able somehow to express herself through look and word and gesture, but his mother herself, her thoughts, her consciousness, her love, her spirit, he never had seen and he never would see. She was the realest force in his life, but she was invisible. When they talked together they signalled to each other out of the unseen where they dwelt. They both were as invisible as God. Moreover, while his mother was only a human, personal spirit, there was a kind of omnipresence in her so far as he was concerned, and he loved her and she loved him everywhere, though he never had seen her and never could. If spiritual life even in its human form can take on such meanings, we need not think of God as an expanded individual in order to love him, be loved by him, and company with him as an unseen friend. Let a man once begin with God as the universal spiritual Presence and then go on to see the divine quality of that Presence revealed in Christ, and there is no limit to the deepening and heightening of his estimation of God's character, except the limits of his own moral imagination.

IV

With many minds the difficulty of achieving an idea of God adequate for our new universe will not be met by any such intellectual shift of emphasis as we have suggested. Not anthropomorphic theology so much as ecclesiasticism is the major burden on their thinking about deity. Two conceptions of the Church are in conflict to-day in modern Protestantism, and one of the most crucial problems of America's religious life in this next generation is the decision as to which of these two ideas of the Church shall triumph. We may call one the exclusive and the other the inclusive conception of the Church. The exclusive conception of the Church lies along lines like these: that we are the true Church; that we have the true doctrines and the true practices as no other Church possesses them; that we are constituted as a Church just because we have these uniquely true opinions and practices; that all we in the Church agree about these opinions and that when we joined the Church we gave allegiance to them; that nobody has any business to belong to our Church unless he agrees with us; that if there are people outside the Church who disagree, they ought to be kept outside and if there are people in the Church who come to disagree, they ought to be put outside. That is the exclusive idea of the Church, and there are many who need no further description of it for they were brought up in it and all their youthful religious life was surrounded by its rigid sectarianism.

Over against this conception is the inclusive idea of the Church, which runs along lines like these: that the Christian Church ought to be the organizing center for all the Christian life of a community; that a Church is not based upon theological uniformity but upon devotion to the Lord Jesus, to the life with God and man for which he stood, and to the work which he gave us to do; that wherever there are people who have that spiritual devotion, who possess that love, who want more of it, who desire to work and worship with those of kindred Christian aspirations, they belong inside the family of the Christian Church. The inclusive idea of the Church looks out upon our American communities and sees there, with all their sin, spiritual life unexpressed and unorganized, good-will and aspiration and moral power unharnessed and going to waste, and it longs to cry so that the whole community can hear it. Come, all men of Christian good-will, let us work together for the Lord of all good life! That is the inclusive idea of the Church. It desires to be the point of incandescence where, regardless of denominationalism or theology, the Christian life of the community bursts into flame.

As between these two conceptions there hardly can be any question that the first idea so far has prevailed. Our endlessly split and shivered Protestantism bears sufficient witness to the influence of the exclusive idea of the Church. The disastrous consequences of this in many realms are evident, and one result lies directly in our argument's path. An exclusive Church narrows the idea of God. Almost inevitably God comes to be conceived as the head of the exclusive Church, the origin of its uniquely true doctrine, the director of its uniquely correct practices, so that the activities of God outside the Church grow dim, and more and more he is conceived as operating through his favourite organization as nowhere else in all the universe. In particular the idea grows easily in the soil of an exclusive Church that God is not operative except in people who recognize him and that the world outside such conscious recognition is largely empty of his activity and barren of his grace. God tends, in such thinking, to become cooped up in the Church, among the people who consciously have acknowledged him. What wonder that multitudes of our youth, waking up to the facts about our vast and growing universe, conclude that it is too big to be managed by the tribal god of a Protestant sect!

The achievement of a worthy idea of God involves, therefore, the ability to discover God in all life, outside the Church as well as within, and in people who do not believe in him nor recognize him as well as in those who do. Let us consider for a moment the principle which is here involved. Many forces and persons serve us when we do not recognize them and do not know the truth about them. This experience of being ministered to by persons whom we do not know goes back even to the maternal care that nourished us before we were born. No mother waits to be recognized before she serves her child. We are tempted to think of persons as ministering to us only when the service is consciously received and acknowledged but, as a matter of fact, service continually comes to us from sources we are unaware of and do not think about.

"Unnumbered comforts to my soul

Thy tender care bestowed,

Before my infant heart conceived

From whom those comforts flowed."

This principle applies to mankind's relationship with the physical universe. Through many generations mankind utterly misconceived it. They thought the earth was flat, the heavens a little way above; yet, for all that, the sun warmed them and the rain refreshed them and the stars guided their wandering boats. The physical universe did not wait until men knew all the truth about it before being useful to men and at last, when the truth came and the glory of this vast and mobile cosmos dawned on mankind, men discovered the facts about forces which, though unknown and unacknowledged, long had served them.

This same principle applies also to man's relationship with social institutions and social securities that have sustained us from our infancy. If a boy knows that there is a Constitution of the United States, he does not think about it. Then maturity comes and he begins vividly to understand the sacrifices which our forefathers underwent in building up the institutions that have nourished us. He recognizes forces and factors of which he had been unconscious but whose value, long unacknowledged, he now gratefully can estimate.

This same principle also applies to our unconscious indebtedness to people who have helped us but whom we have not known. This is a far finer world because of souls who have been here through whom God has shined like the sun through eastern windows, but we can go on year after year absorbing unconsciously the influence of these spirits without ever knowing them. I lived for twelve years in a community to which in its early days a young minister had come, and where for forty years he stood as the central influence in the town's life. He brought it up in the nurture and admonition of the Lord. As was said of Joseph in Potiphar's prison, "Whatsoever they did there, he was the doer of it." The height of his mind, the unselfishness of his spirit, the liberality of his thought, made all the people gladly acclaim him as the foremost citizen of the town. There is a quality in the town's life yet which never would have been there had it not been for him. Sometimes yet his spirit must brood above that community which for forty years he cherished and must say to people whom he never knew, but who are being blessed by the benedictory influence of his life, what Jehovah said to Cyrus the Persian, "I girded thee, though thou hast not known me."

So, from multitudinous sources services flow in upon us that we do not recognize. It should be impossible then to think that God never touches men until men welcome him. Some people seem to suppose that God ministers to men, saves them, transforms them, raises them up and liberates them only when they confessedly receive him. That cannot be true of the God of the New Testament. He is too magnanimous for that. Jesus says a man is unworthy of his discipleship when he serves only the friends who are responsive, that we must serve the hostile and ungrateful, too. Can it be that God is less good than Jesus said we ought to be? We in the churches have drawn our little lines too tight. We have been tempted to divide mankind into two classes, the white and the black: in the Church the white, the saved, who recognize God; outside, the black, the unsaved, the ungodly who do not recognize him. By that division we sometimes seem to imply that those outside the Church are outside the reach of God's transforming grace and power. We are tempted to look for God's activity chiefly, if not altogether, inside the organization that avows him. But that cannot be true. He comes in like the sun through every chink and crevice where he can find a way of entrance. He does not wait to be welcomed. He does not insist on being consciously recognized before he enters a man's life. Rather, through any door or window left unwittingly ajar where he may steal in, even though unobserved, to lift and liberate a life, there the God of the New Testament will come—"the light which lighteth every man coming into the world."

Consider, for illustration, the many people in this generation who have given up active relationship with the Church and assured faith in God. They may even call themselves agnostics. Would it not be true to speak to them like this: You have not succeeded in getting rid of God. There is a flame in your heart that will not go out. You try to say there is no God and then you go out under the stars at night and you begin to wonder how such a vast, law-abiding universe could come by accident, as if a man were to throw a font of type on the floor and by chance it should arrange itself into a play of Shakespeare. Strange universe, without God! You try to say there is no God and you pick up a book: a life of Phillips Brooks or David Livingstone or Francis Xavier, and you begin to wonder that, amid these whirling stars and solar systems, a race of men should have emerged with spiritual life like that which we possess, with ideals that beckon us, conscience that warns us and remorse that punishes us! You cannot easily think that this long spiritual struggle and achievement of the race is an accident struck off unwittingly like sparks from falling stones in a material world without abiding meaning. Or you try to say there is no God, and then you are married and your first baby is born and there wells up in your heart that purest love that man can know, the feeling of a parent for a little child. And you cannot help wondering how a man can walk about the world with love like that in the center of his life, thinking that there is nothing to correspond with it in the reality from which his heart and his baby came. You try to say there is no God, and then you begin to grow old and the friends you love best on earth pass away, as Carlyle said his mother did, like "the last pale rim or sickle of the moon which had once been full, sinking in the dark seas." You cannot help wondering whether great souls can be so at the mercy of a few particles of matter that when these are disturbed the spirit is plunged into oblivion! You never really have gotten rid of God. There is a flame in the center of your heart which you cannot put out. If there were no God it would be easier to disbelieve in him than it is. You cannot get rid of him because the best in you is God in you. The flame is he and there in the center of your life, recognized or unrecognized, he is burning up as best he can.

This principle of God's unrecognized presence applies to a special group of people that has been growing rapidly in the last few years: the men and women who give themselves with high spirit to human service in science or philanthropy but who never think of attributing their service or love of truth to religious motives. To this group belong many of our scientists. They give themselves no rest, seeking for truth which will help human need. In obscure and forgotten laboratories to-day they search for remedies for ancient, lamentable ills. They make it a point of professional honour not to take profit for themselves when they have succeeded, but to give freely to the world the knowledge they have achieved. The pulpit has often quarreled with the scientists. Let the pulpit honour them for their amazing outpouring of service to the world. To this group also belong many of our philanthropists, to whom sacrifice for the common weal has become the moral equivalent of war. Yet often these men and women, useful public servants of the generation as they are, do not know God. They are great spirits. Let us not pretend that they are not. They are making a deep and beneficent impress upon their own times, and our sons and our sons' sons will rise up to call them blessed; yet they do not know God. What are we to say of such men and women? You know what some people do say about them. They use them as arguments against religion. They say, See these fine men living without God. That is an utter fallacy. They are not living without God. They only think they are. They are the supreme examples of the work of the unrecognized God. One wishes that those men and women would recognize God. God can do much more through responsive than through unresponsive lives. But we may not say that they are living without God. There, in the center of their life, in the ideals they work for, in the service they render, in the love they lavish, in the mission that has mastered them, thereis God.

Some time ago I wandered down Broadway, in the small hours of the morning, with one of the prominent citizens of the community. At the heart of his life is the passion to be of use. Because his character is stalwart and his ability great, the scope of his service is far wider than the capacity of most of us. Amid the hurrying crowds and the flashing lights of Broadway we talked together hour after hour about God and immortality. He said that he could not believe in God. He wistfully wished that he could. He was sure that it must add something beautiful to human life, but for himself he thought that there was no possibility except to live a high, clean, serviceable life until he should fall on sleep. All the way home that night I thought of other people whom I know. Here is a man who believes in God. He always has believed in God. He was brought up to believe in God and he has never felt with poignant sympathy enough the abysmal, immedicable woes of human-kind to have his faith disturbed. He never has had any doubts. The war passed over him and left him as it found him. The fiercest storm that ever raged over mankind did not touch the surface of his pool of sheltered faith. How could one help comparing him with my friend who could not believe? For he, in high emotion, had spoken of the miseries of men, of multitudes starving, of the horrors of war, of the poor whose lives are a long animal struggle to keep the body alive, of the woes that fall with such terrific incidence upon the vast, obscure, forgotten masses of our human-kind, and out of the very ardour of his sympathy had cried: "How can you believe that a good Father made a world like this?"

Now, I believe in God with all my heart. But the God whom I believe in likes that man. Jesus, were he here on earth as once he was, would love him. I think Jesus would love him more than the other man who never had faced human misery with sympathy enough to feel his faith disturbed. This does not mean that we ought contentedly to see men ministered to by a God whom they do not recognize. It is a pity to be served by the Eternal Spirit of all grace and yet not know him. In Jean Webster's "Daddy Long Legs," Jerusha Abbott in the orphanage is helped by an unknown friend. Year after year the favours flow in from this friend whom she does not know. She blossoms out into girlhood and young womanhood and still she does not know him. One day she sees him and she does not recognize him.

She has always thought of him as looking other than he does, and so even when she sees him she does not know him. Suppose that the story stopped there! It would be intolerable to have a story end so. To be served all one's life by a friend and then not to know him when he seeks recognition is tragedy. So it is tragedy when God is unrecognized, but behind that is a deeper tragedy still—people who believe in God but who have thoughts of him so narrowly ecclesiastical that they themselves do not perceive his presence, acknowledged or unacknowledged, in all the goodness and truth and beauty of the universe.

Such an enlargement of the idea of God to meet the needs of this new world is one of the innermost demands of religion to-day. When a man believes in the living God as the Creative Power in this universe, whose character was revealed in Christ and who, recognized or unrecognized, reveals himself in every form of goodness, truth and beauty which life anywhere contains, he has achieved a God adequate for life. To such a man the modern progressive outlook upon the world becomes exhilarating; all real advance is a revelation of the purpose of this living God; and, far from being hostile to religion, our modern categories furnish the noblest mental formulae in which the religious spirit ever had opportunity to find expression. We who believe this have no business to be modest and apologetic about it, as though upon the defensive we shyly presented it to the suffrages of men. It is a gospel to proclaim. It does involve a new theology but, with multitudes of eager minds in our generation, the decision no longer lies between an old and a new theology, but between new theology and no theology. No longer can they phrase the deepest experiences of their souls with God in the outgrown categories of a static world. In all their other thinking they live in a world deeply permeated by ideas of progress, and to keep their religion in a separate compartment, uninfluenced by the best knowledge and hope of their day, is an enterprise which, whether it succeed or fail, means the death of vital faith. To take this modern, progressive world into one's mind and then to achieve an idea of God great enough to encompass it, until with the little gods gone and the great God come, life is full of the knowledge of him, as the waters cover the sea, that is alike the duty and the privilege of Christian leadership to-day.

In a world which out of lowly beginnings has climbed so far and seems intended to go on to heights unimagined, God is our hope and in his name we will set up our banners.

9 781835 916353